The Selected Poems of
# Wendell Berry

Also by Wendell Berry

# The Selected Poems of Wendell Berry

COUNTERPOINT

WASHINGTON, D.C.

The author would like to thank the publishers of the following collections from which this selection was made: *The Broken Ground* (1964), *Openings* (1968), *Farming: A Handbook* (1970), *The Country of Marriage* (1973), and *Clearing* (1977) by Harcourt Brace Jovanovich, Inc.; *Findings* (1969) by The Prairie Press; and *A Part* (1980) and *The Wheel* (1982) by North Point / Farrar, Straus & Giroux. Poems from *Entries* (1997) are reprinted by permission of Pantheon Books, a division of Random House, Inc.

*Library of Congress Cataloging-in-Publication Data*
Berry, Wendell, 1934–
The Selected poems of Wendell Berry / Wendell Berry.
    p.    cm.
ISBN 1-887178-84-8 (alk. paper)
1. Country life—Kentucky—Poetry.    2. Farm life—
Kentucky—Poetry.    I. Title
PS3552.E75A6    1998
811'.54—dc21                                98–34793

Book design and electronic composition by David Bullen

Printed in the United States of America on acid-free paper that meets the American National Standards Institute Z39-48 Standard.

COUNTERPOINT
P.O. Box 65793
Washington, D.C. 20035-5793

Counterpoint is a member of the Perseus Books Group.

10  9  8  7  6  5  4  3  2  1

FIRST PRINTING

*from* The Country
of Marriage

For Jack Shoemaker

# CONTENTS

# AUTHOR'S NOTE

I like the idea of a volume of "selected poems" because I like the ideas of culling and condensation and compactness. In making this book, I have culled a lot of poems and thus have achieved some condensation as a matter of course. I might have achieved compactness as well, if I had had the foresight and the good luck to write shorter poems. Having so often failed at brevity, and needing to represent my work at least adequately, I have had to sacrifice compactness in the interest of fairness to myself.

This selection contains none of the poems recently collected in *A Timbered Choir.* To have included work from that book would have made this one *too* large, and would have introduced the problem of representing adequately a distinct body of work.

W. B.

*In a time that breaks*
*in cutting pieces all around,*
*when men, voiceless*
*against thing-ridden men,*
*set themselves on fire, it seems*
*too difficult and rare*
*to think of the life of a man*
*grown whole in the world,*
*at peace and in place.*
*But having thought of it*
*I am beyond the time*
*I might have sold my hands*
*or sold my voice and mind*
*to the arguments of power*
*that go blind against*
*what they would destroy.*

The Selected Poems of
Wendell Berry

*from* The Broken Ground

## THE APPLE TREE
*for Ann and Dick O'Hanlon*

In the essential prose
of things, the apple tree
stands up, emphatic
among the accidents
of the afternoon, solvent,
not to be denied.
The grass has been cut
down, carefully
to leave the orange
poppies still in bloom;
the tree stands up
in the odor of the grass
drying. The forked
trunk and branches are
also a kind of necessary
prose—shingled with leaves,
pigment and song
imposed on the blunt
lineaments of fact, a foliage
of small birds among them.
The tree lifts itself up
in the garden, the
clutter of its green
leaves halving the light,
stating the unalterable
congruity and form
of its casual growth;
the crimson finches appear
and disappear, singing
among the design.

# The Wild

In the empty lot—a place
not natural, but wild—among
the trash of human absence,

the slough and shamble
of the city's seasons, a few
old locusts bloom.

A few woods birds
fly and sing
in the new foliage
—warblers and tanagers, birds
wild as leaves; in a million
each one would be rare,

new to the eyes. A man
couldn't make a habit
of such color,

such flight and singing.
But they are the habit of this
wasted place. In them

the ground is wise. They are
its remembrance of what it is.

# The Plan

My old friend, the owner
of a new boat, stops by
to ask me to fish with him,

and I say I will—both of us
knowing that we may never
get around to it, it may be

years before we're both
idle again on the same day.
But we make a plan, anyhow,

in honor of friendship
and the fine spring weather
and the new boat

and our sudden thought
of the water shining
under the morning fog.

# THE BROKEN GROUND

The opening out and out,
body yielding body:
the breaking
through which the new
comes, perching
above its shadow
on the piling up
darkened broken old
husks of itself:
bud opening to flower
opening to fruit opening
to the sweet marrow
of the seed—
       taken
from what was, from
what could have been.
What is left
is what is.

*from* Findings

# The Design of a House

### 1.

Except in idea, perfection is as wild
as light; there is no hand laid on it.
But the house is a shambles unless
the vision of its perfection
     upholds it like stone.

More probable: the ideal
     of its destruction:
cloud of fire prefiguring
     its disappearance.

What value there is
              is assumed;
like a god, the house elects its omens;
because it is, I desire it should be
—white, its life intact in it,
     among trees.

Love has conceived a house,
and out of its labor
brought forth its likeness
—the emblem of desire, continuing
though the flesh falls away.

### 2.

We've come round again
to short days and long nights;
     time goes;
the clocks barely keep up;

a spare dream of summer
        is kept
alive in the house:

the Queen Anne's lace
        —gobletted,
green beginning to bloom,
tufted, upfurling—
unfolding
        whiteness:

in this winter's memory
more clear than ever in summer,
cold paring away excess:

the single blooming random
in the summer's abundance
of its kind, in high relief
above the clover and grass
of the field, unstill
        an instant,
the day having come upon it,
        green and white
in as much light as ever was.

Opened, white, at the solstice
of its becoming, then the flower
forgets its growing;
        is still;

dirt is its paradigm—
and this memory's seeing,
a cold wind keening the outline.

3.

Winter nights the house sleeps,
a dry seedhead in the snow
falling and fallen, the white
and dark and depth of it, continuing
slow impact of silence.
                            The dark
rooms hold our heads on pillows, waiting
day, through the snow falling and fallen
in the darkness between inconsecutive
dreams. The brain burrows in its earth
and sleeps,
                trusting dawn, though the sun's
light is a light without precedent, never
proved ahead of its coming, waited for
by the law that hope has made it.


4.

What do you intend?
                            Drink blood
and speak, old ghosts. I don't
hear you. What has it amounted to
—the unnegotiable accumulation
of your tears? Your expenditure
has purchased no reprieve. Your
failed wisdom shards among the
down-going atoms of the moment.

History goes blind and in darkness,
neither sees nor is seen, nor is
known except as a carrion
marked with unintelligible wounds;
dragging its dead body, living,

yet to be born, it moves heavily
to its glories. It tramples
the little towns, forgets their names.


5.

If reason were all, reason
would not exist—the will
to reason accounts for it;
it's not reason that chooses
to live; the seed doesn't swell
in its husk by reason, but loves
itself, obeys light which is
its own thought and argues the leaf
in secret; love articulates
the choice of life in fact; life
chooses life because it is
alive; what lives didn't begin dead,
nor sun's fire commence in ember.

Love foresees a jointure
composing a house, a marriage
of contraries, compendium
of opposites in equilibrium.
This morning the sun
came up before the moon set;
shadows were stripped from the house
like burnt rags, the sky turning
blue behind the clear moon,
day and night moving to day.

Let severances be as dividing
budleaves around the flower
—woman and child enfolded, chosen.

It's a dying begun, not lightly,
the taking up of this love
whose legacy is its death.


6.
This is a love poem for you, Tanya—

among wars, among the brutal forfeitures
of time, in this house, among its latent fires,
among all that honesty must see, I accept
your dying, and love you: nothing mitigates
—and for our Mary, chosen by the blind
hungering of our blood, precious and periled
in her happy mornings; whose tears are mine.


7.
There's still a degree of sleep
        recalls
the vast empty dream I slept in
        as a child
sometimes contained a chaos, tangled
like fishline snarled in hooks—
sometimes a hook, whetted, severe,
        drawing
the barbed darkness to a point;
sometimes I seemed merely to be falling.

The house, also, has taken shape in it.


8.
And l have dreamed
of the morning coming in

like a bird through the window
not burdened by a thought,

the light a singing
as I hoped.

It comes in and sings
on the corner of the white washstand,

among coleus stems and roots
in a clear green bottle
on the black tabletop
beneath the window,

under the purple coleus leaves,
among spearing
green philodendron leaves,
on the white washstand:

a small yellow bird with black wings,
darting in and out.


9.
To imagine the thoughtlessness
of a thoughtless thing
is useless.
The mind must sing
of itself to keep awake.

Love has visualized a house,
and out of its expenditure.
fleshed the design
at this cross ways
of consciousness and time:

its form is growth
come to light in it;

croplands, gardens,
are of its architecture,

labor its realization;

solstice is the height
of its consciousness,

thicket a figuration
of its waking;

plants and stars are made convergent
in its windows;

cities we have gone to and come back
are the prospect of its doorways.

And there's a city it dreams of:
salt-white beside the water.

10.
Waking comes into sleep like a dream:
violet dawn over the snow, the black trees.

Snow and the house's white make a white
the black swifts may come back to.

# Three Elegiac Poems

*Harry Erdman Perry, 1881–1965*

## I

Let him escape hospital and doctor,
        the manners and odors of strange places,
        the dispassionate skills of experts.

Let him go free of tubes and needles,
        public corridors, the surgical white
        of life dwindled to poor pain.

Foreseeing the possibility of life without
        possibility of joy, let him give it up.

Let him die in one of the old rooms
        of his living, no stranger near him.

Let him go in peace out of the bodies
        of his life—
        flesh and marriage and household.

From the wide vision of his own windows
        let him go out of sight; and the final

time and light of his life's place be
        last seen before his eyes' slow
        opening in the earth.

Let him go like one familiar with the way
        into the wooded and tracked and
        furrowed hill, his body.

## II

I stand at the cistern in front of the old barn
in the darkness, in the dead of winter,
the night strangely warm, the wind blowing,
rattling an unlatched door.
I draw the cold water up out of the ground, and drink.

At the house the light is still waiting.
An old man I have loved all my life is dying
in his bed there. He is going
slowly down from himself.
In final obedience to his life, he follows
his body out of our knowing.
Only his hands, quiet on the sheet, keep
a painful resemblance to what they no longer are.

## III

He goes free of the earth.
The sun of his last day sets
clear in the sweetness of his liberty.

The earth recovers from his dying,
the hallow of his life remaining
in all his death leaves.

Radiances know him. Grown lighter
than breath, he is set free
in our remembering. Grown brighter

than vision, he goes dark
into the life of the hill
that holds his peace.

He is hidden among all that is,
and cannot be lost.

*from* Openings

# THE THOUGHT OF SOMETHING ELSE

1.

A spring wind blowing
the smell of the ground
through the intersections of traffic,
the mind turns, seeks a new
nativity—another place,
simpler, less weighted
by what has already been.

Another place!
it's enough to grieve me—
that old dream of going,
of becoming a better man
just by getting up and going
to a better place.

2.

The mystery. The old
unaccountable unfolding.
The iron trees in the park
suddenly remember forests.
It becomes possible to think of going

3.

—a place where thought
can take its shape
as quietly in the mind
as water in a pitcher,
or a man can be
safely without thought
—see the day begin

and lean back,
a simple wakefulness filling
perfectly
the spaces among the leaves.


## OCTOBER 10

Now constantly there is the sound,
quieter than rain,
of the leaves falling.

Under their loosening bright
gold, the sycamore limbs
bleach whiter.

Now the only flowers
are beeweed and aster, spray
of their white and lavender
over the brown leaves.

The calling of a crow sounds
loud—a landmark—now
that the life of summer falls
silent, and the nights grow.

# The Winter Rain

The leveling of the water, its increase,
the gathering of many into much:

in the cold dusk I stop
midway of the creek, listening
as it passes downward
loud over the rocks, under
the sound of the rain striking,
nowhere any sound
but the water, the dead
weedstems soaked with it, the
ground soaked, the earth overflowing.

And having waded all the way
across, I look back and see there
on the water the still sky.

# March Snow

The morning lights
whiteness that has touched the world
perfectly as air.
In the whitened country
under the still fall of the snow
only the river, like a brown earth,
taking all falling darkly
into itself, moves.

# The Dream

I dream an inescapable dream
in which I take away from the country
the bridges and roads, the fences, the strung wires,
ourselves, all we have built and dug and hollowed out,
our flocks and herds, our droves of machines.

I restore then the wide-branching trees.
I see growing over the land and shading it
the great trunks and crowns of the first forest.
I am aware of the rattling of their branches,
the lichened channels of their bark, the saps
of the ground flowing upward to their darkness.
Like the afterimage of a light that only by not
looking can be seen, I glimpse the country as it was.
All its beings belong wholly to it. They flourish
in dying as in being born. It is the life of its deaths.

I must end, always, by replacing
our beginning there, ourselves and our blades,
the flowing in of history, putting back what I took away,
trying always with the same pain of foreknowledge
to build all that we have built, but destroy nothing.

My hands weakening, I feel on all sides blindness
growing in the land on its peering bulbous stalks.
I see that my mind is not good enough.
I see that I am eager to own the earth and to own men.
I find in my mouth a bitter taste of money,
a gaping syllable I can neither swallow nor spit out.
I see all that we have ruined in order to have, all
that was owned for a lifetime to be destroyed forever.

Where are the sleeps that escape such dreams?

# The Sycamore

### for Harry Caudill

In the place that is my own place, whose earth
I am shaped in and must bear, there is an old tree growing,
a great sycamore that is a wondrous healer of itself.
Fences have been tied to it, nails driven into it,
hacks and whittles cut in it, the lightning has burned it.
There is no year it has flourished in
that has not harmed it. There is a hollow in it
that is its death, though its living brims whitely
at the lip of the darkness and flows outward.
Over all its scars has come the seamless white
of the bark. It bears the gnarls of its history
healed over. It has risen to a strange perfection
in the warp and bending of its long growth.
It has gathered all accidents into its purpose.
It has become the intention and radiance of its dark fate.
It is a fact, sublime, mystical and unassailable.
In all the country there is no other like it.
I recognize in it a principle, an indwelling
the same as itself, and greater, that I would be ruled by.
I see that it stands in its place, and feeds upon it,
and is fed upon, and is native, and maker.

# DARK WITH POWER

Dark with power, we remain
the invaders of our land, leaving
deserts where forests were,
scars where there were hills.

On the mountains, on the rivers,
on the cities, on the farmlands
we lay weighted hands, our breath
potent with the death of all things.

Pray to us, farmers and villagers
of Vietnam. Pray to us, mothers
and children of helpless countries.
Ask for nothing.

We are carried in the belly
of what we have become
toward the shambles of our triumph,
far from the quiet houses.

Fed with dying, we gaze
on our might's monuments of fire.
The world dangles from us
while we gaze.

# The Want of Peace

All goes back to the earth,
and so I do not desire
pride of excess or power,
but the contentments made
by men who have had little:
the fisherman's silence
receiving the river's grace,
the gardener's musing on rows.

I lack the peace of simple things.
I am never wholly in place.
I find no peace or grace.
We sell the world to buy fire,
our way lighted by burning men,
and that has bent my mind
and made me think of darkness
and wish for the dumb life of roots.

# THE PEACE OF WILD THINGS

When despair for the world grows in me
and I wake in the night at the least sound
in fear of what my life and my children's lives may be,
I go and lie down where the wood drake
rests in his beauty on the water, and the great heron feeds.
I come into the peace of wild things
who do not tax their lives with forethought
of grief. I come into the presence of still water.
And I feel above me the day-blind stars
waiting with their light. For a time
I rest in the grace of the world, and am free.

# GRACE

*for Gurney Norman, quoting him*

The woods is shining this morning.
Red, gold and green, the leaves
lie on the ground, or fall,
or hang full of light in the air still.
Perfect in its rise and in its fall, it takes
the place it has been coming to forever.
It has not hastened here, or lagged.
See how surely it has sought itself,
its roots passing lordly through the earth.
See how without confusion it is
all that it is, and how flawless
its grace is. Running or walking, the way
is the same. Be still. Be still.
"He moves your bones, and the way is clear."

# The Meadow

In the town's graveyard the oldest plot now frees itself
of sorrow, the myrtle of the graves grown wild. The last
who knew the faces who had these names are dead,
and now the names fade, dumb on the stones, wild
as shadows in the grass, clear to the rabbit and the wren.
Ungrieved, the town's ancestry fits the earth. They become
a meadow, their alien marble grown native as maple.

# Marriage
### *to Tanya*

How hard it is for me, who live
in the excitement of women
and have the desire for them
in my mouth like salt. Yet
you have taken me and quieted me.
You have been such light to me
that other women have been
your shadows. You come near me
with the nearness of sleep.
And yet I am not quiet.
It is to be broken. It is to be
torn open. It is not to be
reached and come to rest in
ever. I turn against you,
I break from you, I turn to you.
We hurt, and are hurt,
and have each other for healing.
It is healing. It is never whole.

# Do Not Be Ashamed

You will be walking some night
in the comfortable dark of your yard
and suddenly a great light will shine
round about you, and behind you
will be a wall you never saw before.
It will be clear to you suddenly
that you were about to escape,
and that you are guilty: you misread
the complex instructions, you are not
a member, you lost your card
or never had one. And you will know
that they have been there all along,
their eyes on your letters and books,
their hands in your pockets,
their ears wired to your bed.
Though you have done nothing shameful,
they will want you to be ashamed.
They will want you to kneel and weep
and say you should have been like them.
And once you say you are ashamed,
reading the page they hold out to you,
then such light as you have made
in your history will leave you.
They will no longer need to pursue you.
You will pursue them, begging forgiveness.
They will not forgive you.
There is no power against them.
It is only candor that is aloof from them,
only an inward clarity, unashamed,

that they cannot reach. Be ready.
When their light has picked you out
and their questions are asked, say to them:
"I am not ashamed." A sure horizon
will come around you. The heron will begin
his evening flight from the hilltop.

# Window Poems

#### 1.

Window. Window.
The wind's eye
to see into the wind.
The eye in its hollow
looking out
through the black frame
at the waves the wind
drives up the river,
whitecaps, a wild day,
the white sky
traveled by snow squalls,
the trees thrashing,
the corn blades driven,
quivering, straight out.

#### 2.

The foliage has dropped
below the window's grave edge,
baring the sky, the distant
hills, the branches,
the year's greenness
gone down from the high
light where it so fairly
defied falling.
The country opens to the sky,
the eye purified among hard facts:
the black grid of the window,
the wood of trees branching
outward and outward
to the nervousness of twigs,
buds asleep in the air.

3.

The window has forty
panes, forty clarities
variously wrinkled, streaked
with dried rain, smudged,
dusted. The frame
is a black grid
beyond which the world
flings up the wild
graph of its growth,
tree branch, river,
slope of land,
the river passing
downward, the clouds blowing,
usually, from the west,
the opposite way.
The window is a form
of consciousness, pattern
of formed sense
through which to look
into the wild
that is a pattern too,
but dark and flowing,
bearing along the little
shapes of the mind
as the river bears
a sash of some blinded house.
This windy day
on one of the panes
a blown seed, caught
in cobweb, beats and beats.

4.

This is the wind's eye,
Wendell's window
dedicated to purposes
dark to him, a seeing into
days to come, the winds
of the days as they approach
and go by. He has come
mornings of four years
to be thoughtful here
while day and night
cold and heat
beat upon the world.
In the low room
within the weathers,
sitting at the window,
he has shed himself
at times, and been renewed.
The spark at his wrist
flickers and dies, flickers
and dies.
The life in him
grows and subsides
and grows again
like the icicle throbbing
winter after winter
at a wrinkle in the eave,
flowing over itself
as it comes and goes,
fluid as a branch.


5.

Look in
and see him looking out.

He is not always
quiet, but there have been times
when happiness has come
to him, unasked,
like the stillness on the water
that holds the evening clear
while it subsides
—and he let go
what he was not.
His ancestor is the hill
that rises in the winter wind
beyond the blind wall
at his back.
It wears a patched robe
of some history that he knows
and some that he
does not: healed fields
where the woods comes back
after a time of crops,
human history
done with, a few
ragged fences surviving
among the trees;
and on the ridges still
there are open fields
where the cattle look up
to watch him on his walks
with eyes patient as time.
The hill has known
too many days and men
grown quiet behind him.
But there are mornings
when his soul emerges
from darkness

as out of a hollow in a tree
high on the crest
and takes flight
with savage joy and harsh
outcry down the long slope
of the leaves. And nights
when he sleeps sweating
under the burden of the hill.
At the window
he sits and looks out,
musing on the river,
a little brown hen duck
paddling upstream
among the windwaves
close to the far bank.
What he has understood
lies behind him
like a road in the woods. He is
a wilderness looking out
at the wild.


6.

A warm day in December,
and the rain falling
steadily through the morning
as the man works
at his table, the window
staring into the valley
as though conscious
when he is not. The cold river
steams in the warm air.
It is rising. Already
the lowest willows
stand in the water

and the swift currents
fold round them.
The bare twigs of the elms
are beaded with bright drops
that grow slowly heavy
and fall, bigger
and slower than the raindrops.
A fox squirrel comes
through the trees, hurrying
someplace, but it seems
to be raining everywhere,
and he submits to wetness
and sits still, miserable
maybe, for an hour.
How sheltering and clear
the window seems, the dry fireheat
inside, and outside the gray
downpour. As the man works
the weather moves
upon his mind, its dreariness
a kind of comfort.


7.

Outside the window
is a roofed wooden tray
he fills with seeds for the birds.
They make a sort of dance
as they descend and light
and fly off at a slant
across the strictly divided
black sash. At first
they came fearfully, worried
by the man's movements
inside the room. They watched

his eyes, and flew
when he looked. Now they expect
no harm from him
and forget he's there.
They come into his vision,
unafraid. He keeps
a certain distance and quietness
in tribute to them.
That they ignore him
he takes in tribute to himself.
But they stay cautious
of each other, half afraid, unwilling
to be too close. They snatch
what they can carry and fly
into the trees. They flirt out
with tail or beak and waste
more sometimes than they eat.
And the man, knowing
the price of seed, wishes
they would take more care.
But they understand only
what is free, and he
can give only as they
will take. Thus they have
enlightened him. He buys
the seed, to make it free.

8.

The river is rising,
approaching the window
in awful nearness.
Over it the air holds
a tense premonition
of the water's dark body

living where yesterday
things breathed. As he works
through the morning
the man has trouble
in the corner of his eye,
whole trees turning
in the channel as they go by,
the currents loaded
with the trash of the woods
and the trash of towns,
bearing down, and rising.


9.

There is a sort of vertical
geography that portions his life.
Outside, the chickadees
and titmice scrounge
his sunflower seed. The cardinals
feed like fires on mats of drift
lying on the currents
of the swollen river.
The air is a bridge
and they are free. He imagines
a necessary joy
in things that must fly
to eat. He is set apart
by the black grid of the window
and, below it, the table
of the contents of his mind:
notes and remnants,
uncompleted work,
unanswered mail,
unread books
—the subjects of conscience,

his yoke-fellow,
whose whispered accounting
has stopped one ear, leaving him
half deaf to the world.
Some pads of paper,
eleven pencils,
a leaky pen,
a jar of ink
are his powers. He'll
never fly.


10.

Rising, the river
is wild. There is no end
to what one may imagine
whose lands and buildings
lie in its reach. To one
who has felt his little boat
taken this way and that
in the braided currents
it is beyond speech.
"What's the river doing?"
"Coming up."
In Port Royal, that begins
a submergence of minds.
Heads are darkened.
To the man at work
through the mornings
in the long-legged cabin
above the water, there is
an influence of the rise
that he feels in his footsoles
and in his belly
even while he thinks

of something else. The window
looks out, like a word,
upon the wordless, fact
dissolving into mystery, darkness
overtaking light.
And the water reaches a height
it can only fall from, leaving
the tree trunks wet.
It has made a roof
to its rising, and become
a domestic thing.
It lies down in its place
like a horse in his stall.
Facts emerge from it:
drift it has hung in the trees,
stranded cans and bottles,
new carving in the banks
—a place of change, changed.
It leaves a mystic plane
in the air, a membrane
of history stretched between
the silt-lines on the banks,
a depth that for months
the man will go from his window
down into, knowing
he goes within the reach
of a dark power: where
the birds are, fish
were.

II.
How fine
to have a long-legged house
with a many-glassed window

looking out on the river
—and the wren singing
on a winter morning! How fine
to sweep the floor,
opening the doors
to let the air change,
and then to sit down
in the freshened room,
day pouring in the window!
But this is only for a while.
This house was not always
here. Another stood
in its place, and weathered
and grew old. He tore it down
and used the good of it
to build this. And farther on
another stood
that is gone. Nobody
alive now knows
how it looked, though some
recall a springhouse
that is gone too now. The stones
strew the pasture grass
where a roan colt grazes
and lifts his head to snort
at commotions in the wind.
All passes, and the man
at work in the house
has mostly ceased to mind.
There will be pangs
of ending, and he regrets
the terrors men bring to men.
But all passes—there is even
a kind of solace in that.

He has imagined animals
grazing at nightfall
on the place where his house stands.
Already his spirit
is with them, with a strange attentiveness,
hearing the grass
quietly tearing as they graze.

12.

The country where he lives
is haunted
by the ghost of an old forest.
In the cleared fields
where he gardens
and pastures his horses
it stood once,
and will return. There will be
a resurrection of the wild.
Already it stands in wait
at the pasture fences.
It is rising up
in the waste places of the cities.
When the fools of the capitals
have devoured each other
in righteousness,
and the machines have eaten
the rest of us, then
there will be the second coming
of the trees. They will come
straggling over the fences
slowly, but soon enough.
The highways will sound
with the feet of the wild herds,
returning. Beaver will ascend

the streams as the trees
close over them.
The wolf and the panther
will find their old ways
through the nights. Water
and air will flow clear.
Certain calamities
will have passed,
and certain pleasures.
The wind will do without
corners. How difficult
to think of it: miles and miles
and no window.


13.

Sometimes he thinks the earth
might be better without humans.
He's ashamed of that.
It worries him,
him being a human, and needing
to think well of the others
in order to think well of himself.
And there are
a few he thinks well of,
a few he loves
as well as himself almost,
and he would like to say
better. But history
is so largely unforgivable.
And now his mighty government
wants to help everybody
even if it has to kill them
to do it—like the fellow in the story
who helped his neighbor to Heaven:

"I heard the Lord calling him,
Judge, and I sent him on."
According to the government
everybody is just waiting
to be given a chance
to be like us. He can't
go along with that.
Here is a thing, flesh of his flesh,
that he hates. He would like
a little assurance
that no one will destroy the world
for some good cause.
Until he dies, he would like his life
to pertain to the earth.
But there is something in him
that will wait, even
while he protests,
for things to turn out as they will.
Out his window this morning
he saw nine ducks in flight,
and a hawk dive at his mate
in delight.
The day stands apart
from the calendar. There is a will
that receives it as enough.
He is given a fragment of time
in this fragment of the world.
He likes it pretty well.


    14.
The longest night is past.
It is the blessed morning of the year.
Beyond the window, snow
in patches on the river bank,

frosty sunlight on the dry corn,
and buds on the water maples
red, red in the cold.


15.
The sycamore gathers
out of the sky, white
in the glance that looks up to it
through the black crisscross
of the window. But it is not a glance
that it offers itself to.
It is no lightning stroke
caught in the eye. It stays,
an old holding in place.
And its white is not so pure
as a glance would have it,
but emerges partially,
the tree's renewal of itself,
among the mottled browns
and olives of the old bark.
Its dazzling comes into the sun
a little at a time
as though a god in it
is slowly revealing himself.
How often the man of the window
has studied its motley trunk,
the out-starting of its branches,
its smooth crotches,
its revelations of whiteness,
hoping to see beyond his glances,
the distorting geometry
of preconception and habit,
to know it beyond words.
All he has learned of it

does not add up to it.
There is a bird who nests in it
in the summer and seems to sing of it—
the quick lights among its leaves
—better than he can.
It is not by his imagining
its whiteness comes.
The world is greater than our words.
To speak of it the mind must bend.


16.

His mind gone from the window
into dark thought, suddenly
a flash of water
lights in the corner of his eye:
the kingfisher is rising,
laden, out of his plunge,
the water still subsiding
under the bare willow.
The window becomes a part
of his mind's history, the entrance
of days into it. And awake
now, watching the water flow
beyond the glass, his mind
is watched by a spectre of itself
that is a window on the past.
Life steadily adding
its subtractions, it has fallen
to him to remember
an old man who, dying,
dreamed of his garden,
a harvest so bountiful
he could not carry it home
—another who saw

in the flaws of the moon
a woman's face
like a cameo.


17.
For a night and a day
his friend stayed here
on his way across the continent.
In the afternoon they walked
down from Port Royal
to the river, following
for a while the fall of Camp Branch
through the woods,
then crossing the ridge
and entering the woods again
on the valley rim. They talked
of history—men who saw visions
of crops where the trees stood
and stand again, the crops
gone. They ate the cold apples
they carried in their pockets.
They lay on a log in the sun
to rest, looking up
through bare branches at the sky.
They saw a nuthatch walk
in a loop on the side of a tree
in a late patch of light
while below them the *Lexington*
shoved sand up the river,
her diesels shaking the air.
They walked along trees
across ravines. Now his friend
is back on the highway, and he sits again

at his window. Another day.
During the night snow fell.

18.
The window grows fragile
in a time of war.
The man seated beneath it
feels its glass turn deadly.
He feels the nakedness
of his face and throat.
Its shards and splinters balance
in transparence, delicately
seamed. In the violence
of men against men, it will not last.
In any mind turned away
in hate, it will go blind.
Men spare one another
by will. When there is hate
it is joyous to kill. And he
has borne the hunger to destroy,
riding anger like a captain,
savage, exalted and blind.
There is war in his veins
like a loud song.
He has known his heart to rise
in glad holocaust against his kind,
and felt hard in thigh and arm
the thew of fury.

19.
Peace. May he waken
not too late from his wraths
to find his window still

clear in its wall, and the world
there. Within things
there is peace, and at the end
of things. It is the mind
turned away from the world
that turns against it.
The armed presidents stand
on deadly islands in the air,
overshadowing the crops.
Peace. Let men, who cannot be brothers
to themselves, be brothers
to mulleins and daisies
that have learned to live on the earth.
Let them understand the pride
of sycamores and thrushes
that receive the light gladly, and do not
think to illuminate themselves.
Let them know that the foxes and the owls
are joyous in their lives,
and their gayety is praise to the heavens,
and they do not raven with their minds.
In the night the devourer,
and in the morning all things
find the light a comfort.
Peace. The earth turns
against all living, in the end.
And when mind has not outraged
itself against its nature,
they die and become the place
they lived in. Peace to the bones
that walk in the sun toward death,
for they will come to it soon enough.
Let the phoebes return in spring
and build their nest of moss

in the porch rafters,
and in autumn let them depart.
Let the garden be planted,
and let the frost come.
Peace to the porch and the garden.
Peace to the man in the window.


20.

In the early morning dark
he dreamed of the spring woodsflowers
standing in the ground,
dark yet under the leaves and under
the bare cold branches.
But in his dream he knew their way
was prepared, and in their time
they would rise up joyful.
And though he had dreamed earlier
of strife, his sleep became peaceful.
He said: If we, who have killed
our brothers and hated ourselves,
are made in the image of God,
then surely the bloodroot,
wild phlox, trillium, and mayapple
are more truly made
in God's image, for they have desired
to be no more than they are,
and they have spared each other.
Their future
is undiminished by their past.
Let me, he said in his dream,
become always less a soldier
and more a man,
for what is unopened in the ground
is pledged to peace.

When he woke and went out
a flock of wild ducks that had fed
on the river while he slept
flew off in fear of him.
And he walked, manly, into the new day.
He came to his window
where he sat and looked out,
the earth before him, blessed
by his dream of peace,
bad history behind him.


21.

He has known a tunnel
through the falling snow
that brought him back at dark
and nearly killed him on the way,
the road white as the sky
and the snow piling.
Mortality crept up close
in the darkness round his eyes.
He felt his death's wrenched avatars
lying like silent animals
along the ditch. He thought
of his wife, his supper and his bed,
and kept on, and made it.
Now he sits at the window
again, the country hard and bright
in this winter's coldest morning.
The river, unfrozen still,
gives off a breath of smoke
that flows upstream with the wind.
Behind him that burrow
along the wild road
grows certain in his mind,

leading here, surely. It has arrived
at the window, and is clarified.
Now he has learned another way
he can come here. Luck
taught him, and desire.
The snow lies under the woods
and February is ending.
Far off, another way, he hears
the flute of spring,
an old-style traveler,
wandering through the trees.

22.

Still sleeping, he heard
the phoebe call, and woke to it,
and winter passed out of his mind.
The bird, in the high branches
above the road-culvert mouth,
sang to what was sleeping,
two notes, clear and
harsh. The stream came,
full-voiced, down the rocks
out of the woods. The wood ducks
have come back to nest
in the old hollow sycamore.
The window has changed, no longer
remembering, but waiting.

23.

He stood on the ground
and saw his wife borne away
in the air, and suddenly
knew her. It is not the sky
he trusts her to, or her flight,

but to herself as he saw her
turn back and smile. And he
turned back to the buried garden
where the spring flood rose.
The window is made strange
by these days he has come to.
She is the comfort of the rooms
she leaves behind her.


24.

His love returns
and walks among the trees,
a new time lying beneath
the leaves at her feet.
There are songs in the ground
audible to her. She enters
the dark globe of sleep,
waking the tree frogs
whose songs star the silence
in constellations. She wakens
the birds of mornings. The sun
makes a low gentle piping.
The bloodroot rises in its folded
leaf, and there is a tensing
in the woods. There is
no window where she is.
All is clear where the light begins
to dress the branch in green.


25.

The bloodroot is white
in the woods, and men renew
their abuse of the world
and each other. Abroad

we burn and maim
in the name of principles
we no longer recognize in acts.
At home our flayed land
flows endlessly
to burial in the sea.
When mortality is not heavy
on us, humanity is—
public meaninglessness
preying on private meaning.
As the weather warms, the driven
swarm into the river,
pursued by whining engines,
missing the world
as they pass over it,
every man
his own mosquito.

26.

In the heron's eye
is one of the dies of change.
Another
is in the sun.
Each thing is carried
beyond itself.
The man of the window
lives at the edge,
knowing the approach
of what must be, joy
and dread.
Now the old sycamore
yields at its crown
a dead branch.
It will sink like evening

into its standing place.
The young trees rise,
and the dew is on them,
and the heat of the day
is on them, and the dark
—end and beginning
without end.

27.

Now that April with sweet rain
has come to Port Royal again,
Burley Coulter rows out
on the river to fish.
He sits all day in his boat,
tied to a willow, his hat
among green branches,
his dark line curving
in the wind. He is one
with the sun.
The current's horses graze
in the shade along the banks.
The watcher leaves his window
and goes out.
He sits in the woods, watched
by more than he sees.
What is his is
past. He has come
to a roofless place
and a windowless.
There is a wild light
his mind loses
until the spring renews,
but it holds his mind
and will not let it rest.

The window is a fragment
of the world suspended
in the world, the known
adrift in mystery.
And now the green
rises. The window has an edge
that is celestial,
where the eyes are surpassed.

# To a Siberian Woodsman

*(after looking at some pictures in a magazine)*

### 1.

You lean at ease in your warm house at night after supper,
listening to your daughter play the accordion. You smile
with the pleasure of a man confident in his hands, resting
after a day of long labor in the forest, the cry of the saw
in your head, and the vision of coming home to rest.
Your daughter's face is clear in the joy of hearing
her own music. Her fingers live on the keys
like people familiar with the land they were born in.

You sit at the dinner table late into the night with your son,
tying the bright flies that will lead you along the forest streams.
Over you, as your hands work, is the dream of the still pools.
     Over you is the dream
of your silence while the east brightens, birds waking close by
     you in the trees.

### 2.

I have thought of you stepping out of your doorway at dawn,
     your son in your tracks.
You go in under the overarching green branches of the forest
whose ways, strange to me, are well known to you as the sound
     of your own voice
or the silence that lies around you now that you have ceased to
     speak,
and soon the voice of the stream rises ahead of you, and you
     take the path beside it.
I have thought of the sun breaking pale through the mists over
     you

as you come to the pool where you will fish, and of the mist
      drifting
over the water, and of the cast fly resting light on the face of the
      pool.


3.

And I am here in Kentucky in the place I have made myself
in the world. I sit on my porch above the river that flows muddy
and slow along the feet of the trees. I hear the voices of the wren
and the yellow-throated warbler whose songs pass near the
      windows
and over the roof. In my house my daughter learns the
      womanhood
of her mother. My son is at play, pretending to be
the man he believes I am. I am the outbreathing of this ground.
My words are its words as the wren's song is its song.


4.

Who has invented our enmity? Who has prescribed us
hatred of each other? Who has armed us against each other
with the death of the world? Who has appointed me such anger
that I should desire the burning of your house or the
      destruction of your children?
Who has appointed such anger to you? Who has set loose the
      thought
that we should oppose each other with the ruin of forests and
      rivers, and the silence of birds?
Who has said to us that the voices of my land shall be strange
to you, and the voices of your land strange to me?

Who has imagined that I would destroy myself in order to
      destroy you,

or that I could improve myself by destroying you? Who has
     imagined
that your death could be negligible to me now that I have seen
     these pictures of your face?
Who has imagined that I would not speak familiarly with you,
or laugh with you, or visit in your house and go to work with
     you in the forest?
And now one of the ideas of my place will be that you would
     gladly talk and visit and work with me.


     5.

I sit in the shade of the trees of the land I was born in.
As they are native I am native, and I hold to this place as
     carefully as they hold to it.
I do not see the national flag flying from the staff of the
     sycamore,
or any decree of the government written on the leaves of the
     walnut,
nor has the elm bowed before monuments or sworn the oath of
     allegiance.
They have not declared to whom they stand in welcome.


     6.

In the thought of you I imagine myself free of the weapons and
     the official hates that I have borne on my back like a
     hump,
and in the thought of myself I imagine you free of weapons and
     official hates,
so that if we should meet we would not go by each other
     looking at the ground like slaves sullen under their
     burdens,
but would stand clear in the gaze of each other.

7.

There is no government so worthy as your son who fishes with
    you in silence beside the forest pool.

There is no national glory so comely as your daughter whose
    hands have learned a music and go their own way on the
    keys.

There is no national glory so comely as my daughter who
    dances and sings and is the brightness of my house.

There is no government so worthy as my son who laughs, as he
    comes up the path from the river in the evening, for joy.

# A Discipline

Turn toward the holocaust, it approaches
on every side, there is no other place
to turn. Dawning in your veins
is the light of the blast
that will print your shadow on stone
in a last antic of despair
to survive you in the dark.
Man has put his history to sleep
in the engine of doom. It flies
over his dreams in the night,
a blazing cocoon. O gaze into the fire
and be consumed with man's despair,
and be still, and wait. And then see
the world go on with the patient work
of seasons, embroidering birdsong
upon itself as for a wedding, and feel
your heart set out in the morning
like a young traveler, arguing the world
from the kiss of a pretty girl.
It is the time's discipline to think
of the death of all living, and yet live.

*from* Farming: A Handbook

# The Man Born to Farming

The grower of trees, the gardener, the man born to farming,
whose hands reach into the ground and sprout,
to him the soil is a divine drug. He enters into death
yearly, and comes back rejoicing. He has seen the light lie down
in the dung heap, and rise again in the corn.
His thought passes along the row ends like a mole.
What miraculous seed has he swallowed
that the unending sentence of his love flows out of his mouth
like a vine clinging in the sunlight, and like water
descending in the dark?

# February 2, 1968

In the dark of the moon, in flying snow, in the dead of winter,
war spreading, families dying, the world in danger,
I walk the rocky hillside, sowing clover.

## The Stones

I owned a slope full of stones.
Like buried pianos they lay in the ground,
shards of old sea-ledges, stumbling blocks
where the earth caught and kept them
dark, an old music mute in them
that my head keeps now I have dug them out.
I broke them where they slugged in their dark
cells, and lifted them up in pieces.
As I piled them in the light
I began their music. I heard their old lime
rouse in breath of song that has not left me.
I gave pain and weariness to their bearing out.
What bond have I made with the earth,
having worn myself against it? It is a fatal singing
I have carried with me out of that day.
The stones have given me music
that figures for me their holes in the earth
and their long lying in them dark.
They have taught me the weariness that loves the ground,
 and I must prepare a fitting silence.




## To Know the Dark

To go in the dark with a light is to know the light.
To know the dark, go dark. Go without sight,
and find that the dark, too, blooms and sings,
and is traveled by dark feet and dark wings.

## The Supplanting

Where the road came, no longer bearing men,
but briars, honeysuckle, buckbush and wild grape,
the house fell to ruin, and only the old wife's daffodils
rose in spring among the wild vines to be domestic
and to keep the faith, and her peonies drenched the tangle
with white bloom. For a while in the years of its wilderness
a wayfaring drunk slept clinched to the floor there
in the cold nights. And then I came, and set fire
to the remnants of house and shed, and let time
hurry in the flame. I fired it so that all
would burn, and watched the blaze settle on the waste
like a shawl. I knew those old ones departed
then, and I arrived. As the fire fed, I felt rise in me
something that would not bear my name—something that
        bears us
through the flame, and is lightened of us, and is glad.


## The Springs

In a country without saints or shrines
I knew one who made his pilgrimage
to springs, where in his life's dry years
his mind held on. Everlasting,
people called them, and gave them names.
The water broke into sounds and shinings
at the vein mouth, bearing the taste
of the place, the deep rock, sweetness
out of the dark. He bent and drank
in bondage to the ground.

# THE WISH TO BE GENEROUS

All that I serve will die, all my delights,
the flesh kindled from my flesh, garden and field,
the silent lilies standing in the woods,
the woods, the hill, the whole earth, all
will burn in man's evil, or dwindle
in its own age. Let the world bring on me
the sleep of darkness without stars, so I may know
my little light taken from me into the seed
of the beginning and the end, so I may bow
to mystery, and take my stand on the earth
like a tree in a field, passing without haste
or regret toward what will be, my life
a patient willing descent into the grass.

# A PRAISE

His memories lived in the place
like fingers locked in the rock ledges
like roots. When he died
and his influence entered the air
I said, Let my mind be the earth
of his thought, let his kindness
go ahead of me. Though I do not escape
the history barbed in my flesh,
certain wise movements of his hands,
the turns of his speech
keep with me. His hope of peace
keeps with me in harsh days,
the shell of his breath dimming away
three summers in the earth.

# Enriching the Earth

To enrich the earth I have sowed clover and grass
to grow and die. I have plowed in the seeds
of winter grains and of various legumes,
their growth to be plowed in to enrich the earth.
I have stirred into the ground the offal
and the decay of the growth of past seasons
and so mended the earth and made its yield increase.
All this serves the dark. I am slowly falling
into the fund of things. And yet to serve the earth,
not knowing what I serve, gives a wideness
and a delight to the air, and my days
do not wholly pass. It is the mind's service,
for when the will fails so do the hands
and one lives at the expense of life.
After death, willing or not, the body serves,
entering the earth. And so what was heaviest
and most mute is at last raised up into song.

## AIR AND FIRE

From my wife and household and fields
that I have so carefully come to in my time
I enter the craziness of travel,
the reckless elements of air and fire.
Having risen up from my native land,
I find myself smiled at by beautiful women,
making me long for a whole life
to devote to each one, making love to her
in some house, in some way of sleeping
and waking I would make only for her.
And all over the country I find myself
falling in love with houses, woods, and farms
that I will never set foot in.
My eyes go wandering through America,
two wayfaring brothers, resting in silence
against the forbidden gates. O what if
an angel came to me, and said,
"Go free of what you have done. Take
what you want." The atoms of blood
and brain and bone strain apart
at the thought. What I am is the way home.
Like rest after a sleepless night,
my old love comes on me in midair.

# A STANDING GROUND

*Flee fro the prees, and dwelle with sothfastnesse;*
*Suffyce unto thy thyng, though hit be smal...*

However just and anxious I have been,
I will stop and step back
from the crowd of those who may agree
with what I say, and be apart.
There is no earthly promise of life or peace
but where the roots branch and weave
their patient silent passages in the dark;
uprooted, I have been furious without an aim.
I am not bound for any public place,
but for ground of my own
where I have planted vines and orchard trees,
and in the heat of the day climbed up
into the healing shadow of the woods.
Better than any argument is to rise at dawn
and pick dew-wet red berries in a cup.

# Song in a Year of Catastrophe

I began to be followed by a voice saying:
"It can't last. It can't last.
Harden yourself. Harden yourself.
Be ready. Be ready."

"Go look under the leaves,"
it said, "for what is living there
is long dead in your tongue."
And it said, "Put your hands
into the earth. Live close
to the ground. Learn the darkness.
Gather round you all
the things that you love, name
their names, prepare
to lose them. It will be
as if all you know were turned
around within your body."

And I went and put my hands
into the ground, and they took root
and grew into a season's harvest.
I looked behind the veil
of the leaves, and heard voices
that I knew had been dead
in my tongue years before my birth.
I learned the dark.

And still the voice stayed with me.
Waking in the early mornings,
I could hear it, like a bird
bemused among the leaves,

a mockingbird idly singing
in the autumn of catastrophe:

"Be ready. Be ready.
Harden yourself. Harden yourself."

And I heard the sound
of a great engine pounding
in the air, and a voice asking:
"Change or slavery?
Hardship or slavery?"
and voices answering:
"Slavery! Slavery!"
And I was afraid, loving
what I knew would be lost.

Then the voice following me said:
"You have not yet come close enough.
Come nearer the ground. Learn
from the woodcock in the woods
whose feathering is a ritual
of the fallen leaves,
and from the nesting quail
whose speckling makes her hard to see
in the long grass.
Study the coat of the mole.
For the farmer shall wear
the furrows and the greenery
of his fields, and bear
the long standing of the woods."

And I asked: "You mean death, then?"
"Yes," the voice said. "Die

into what the earth requires of you."
I let go all holds then, and sank
like a hopeless swimmer into the earth,
and at last came fully into the ease
and the joy of that place,
all my lost ones returning.

*9.28.68*


# The Current

Having once put his hand into the ground,
seeding there what he hopes will outlast him,
a man has made a marriage with his place,
and if he leaves it his flesh will ache to go back.
His hand has given up its birdlife in the air.
It has reached into the dark like a root
and begun to wake, quick and mortal, in timelessness,
a flickering sap coursing upward into his head
so that he sees the old tribespeople bend
in the sun, digging with sticks, the forest opening
to receive their hills of corn, squash, and beans,
their lodges and graves, and closing again.
He is made their descendant, what they left
in the earth rising into him like a seasonal juice.
And he sees the bearers of his own blood arriving,
the forest burrowing into the earth as they come,
their hands gathering the stones up into walls,
and relaxing, the stones crawling back into the ground
to lie still under the black wheels of machines.
The current flowing to him through the earth
flows past him, and he sees one descended from him,
a young man who has reached into the ground,
his hand held in the dark as by a hand.

# Meditation in the Spring Rain

In the April rain I climbed up to drink
of the live water leaping off the hill,
white over the rocks. Where the mossy root
of a sycamore cups the flow, I drank
and saw the branches feathered with green.
The thickets, I said, send up their praise
at dawn. Was that what I meant—I meant
my words to have the heft and grace, the flight
and weight of the very hill, its life
rising—or was it some old exultation
that abides with me? We'll not soon escape
the faith of our fathers—no more than
crazy old Mrs. Gaines, whom my grandmother
remembers standing balanced eighty years ago
atop a fence in Port Royal, Kentucky,
singing: "One Lord, one Faith, and one
Cornbread." They had a cage built for her
in a room, "nearly as big as the room, not
cramped up," and when she grew wild
they kept her there. But mostly she went free
in the town, and they allowed the children
to go for walks with her. She strayed once
beyond where they thought she went, was lost
to them, "and they had an awful time
finding her." For her, to be free
was only to be lost. What is it about her
that draws me on, so that my mind becomes a child
to follow after her? An old woman
when my grandmother was a girl, she must have seen
the virgin forest standing here, the amplitude
of our beginning, of which no speech
remains. Out of the town's lost history,
buried in minds long buried, she has come,

brought back by a memory near death. I see her
in her dusky clothes, hair uncombed, the children
following. I see her wandering, muttering
to herself as her way was, among these hills
half a century before my birth, in the silence
of such speech as I know. Dawn and twilight
and dawn again trembling in the leaves
over her, she tramped the raveling verges
of her time. It was a shadowy country
that she knew, holding a darkness that was past
and a darkness to come. The fleeting lights
tattered her churchly speech to mad song.
When her poor wandering head broke the confines
of all any of them knew, they put her in a cage.
But I am glad to know it was a commodious cage,
not cramped up. And I am glad to know
that other times the town left her free
to be as she was in it, and to go her way.
May it abide a poet with as much grace!
For I too am perhaps a little mad,
standing here wet in the drizzle, listening
to the clashing syllables of the water. Surely
there is a great Word being put together here.
I begin to hear it gather in the opening
of the flowers and the leafing-out of the trees,
in the growth of bird nests in the crotches
of the branches, in the settling of the dead
leaves into the ground, in the whittling
of beetle and grub, in my thoughts
moving in the hill's flesh. Coming here,
I crossed a place where a stream flows
underground, and the sounds of the hidden water
and the water come to light braided in my ear.

I think the maker is here, creating his hill
as it will be, out of what it was.
The thickets, I say, send up their praise
at dawn! One Lord, one Faith, and one Cornbread
forever! But hush. Wait. Be as still
as the dead and the unborn in whose silence
that old one walked, muttering and singing,
followed by the children.

                    For a time there
I turned away from the words I knew, and was lost.
For a time I was lost and free, speechless
in the multitudinous assembling of his Word.

# TO THE UNSEEABLE ANIMAL

My daughter: *"I hope there's an animal
somewhere that nobody has ever seen.
And I hope nobody ever sees it."*

Being, whose flesh dissolves
at our glance, knower
of the secret sums and measures,
you are always here,
dwelling in the oldest sycamores,
visiting the faithful springs
when they are dark and the foxes
have crept to their edges.
I have come upon pools
in streams, places overgrown
with the woods' shadow,
where I knew you had rested,
watching the little fish
hang still in the flow;
as I approached they seemed
particles of your clear mind
disappearing among the rocks.
I have waked deep in the woods
in the early morning, sure
that while I slept
your gaze passed over me.
That we do not know you
is your perfection
and our hope. The darkness
keeps us near you.

## Breaking

Did I believe I had a clear mind?
It was like the water of a river
flowing shallow over the ice. And now
that the rising water has broken
the ice, I see that what I thought
was the light is part of the dark.


## Prayer after Eating

I have taken in the light
that quickened eye and leaf.
May my brain be bright with praise
of what I eat, in the brief blaze
of motion and of thought.
May I be worthy of my meat.

# The Country of Marriage

### 1.

I dream of you walking at night along the streams
of the country of my birth, warm blooms and the nightsongs
of birds opening around you as you walk.
You are holding in your body the dark seed of my sleep.

### 2.

This comes after silence. Was it something I said
that bound me to you, some mere promise
or, worse, the fear of loneliness and death?
A man lost in the woods in the dark, I stood
still and said nothing. And then there rose in me,
like the earth's empowering brew rising
in root and branch, the words of a dream of you
I did not know I had dreamed. I was a wanderer
who feels the solace of his native land
under his feet again and moving in his blood.
I went on, blind and faithful. Where I stepped
my track was there to steady me. It was no abyss
that lay before me, but only the level ground.

### 3.

Sometimes our life reminds me
of a forest in which there is a graceful clearing
and in that opening a house,
an orchard and garden,
comfortable shades, and flowers
red and yellow in the sun, a pattern
made in the light for the light to return to.
The forest is mostly dark, its ways
to be made anew day after day, the dark

richer than the light and more blessed,
provided we stay brave
enough to keep on going in.


4.

How many times have I come to you out of my head
with joy, if ever a man was,
for to approach you I have given up the light
and all directions. I come to you
lost, wholly trusting as a man who goes
into the forest unarmed. It is as though I descend
slowly earthward out of the air. I rest in peace
in you, when I arrive at last.


5.

Our bond is no little economy based on the exchange
of my love and work for yours, so much for so much
of an expendable fund. We don't know what its limits are—
that puts it in the dark. We are more together
than we know, how else could we keep on discovering
we are more together than we thought?
You are the known way leading always to the unknown,
and you are the known place to which the unknown is always
leading me back. More blessed in you than I know,
I possess nothing worthy to give you, nothing
not belittled by my saying that I possess it.
Even an hour of love is a moral predicament, a blessing
a man may be hard up to be worthy of. He can only
accept it, as a plant accepts from all the bounty of the light
enough to live, and then accepts the dark,
passing unencumbered back to the earth, as I
have fallen time and again from the great strength
of my desire, helpless, into your arms.

6.

What I am learning to give you is my death
to set you free of me, and me from myself
into the dark and the new light. Like the water
of a deep stream, love is always too much. We
did not make it. Though we drink till we burst
we cannot have it all, or want it all.
In its abundance it survives our thirst.
In the evening we come down to the shore
to drink our fill, and sleep, while it
flows through the regions of the dark.
It does not hold us, except we keep returning
to its rich waters thirsty. We enter,
willing to die, into the commonwealth of its joy.


7.

I give you what is unbounded, passing from dark to dark,
containing darkness: a night of rain, an early morning.
I give you the life I have let live for love of you:
a clump of orange-blooming weeds beside the road,
the young orchard waiting in the snow, our own life
that we have planted in this ground, as I
have planted mine in you. I give you my love for all
beautiful and honest women that you gather to yourself
again and again, and satisfy—and this poem,
no more mine than any man's who has loved a woman.

# Manifesto: The Mad Farmer Liberation Front

Love the quick profit, the annual raise,
vacation with pay. Want more
of everything ready-made. Be afraid
to know your neighbors and to die.
And you will have a window in your head.
Not even your future will be a mystery
any more. Your mind will be punched in a card
and shut away in a little drawer.
When they want you to buy something
they will call you. When they want you
to die for profit they will let you know.
So, friends, every day do something
that won't compute. Love the Lord.
Love the world. Work for nothing.
Take all that you have and be poor.
Love someone who does not deserve it.
Denounce the government and embrace
the flag. Hope to live in that free
republic for which it stands.
Give your approval to all you cannot
understand. Praise ignorance, for what man
has not encountered he has not destroyed.
Ask the questions that have no answers.
Invest in the millennium. Plant sequoias.
Say that your main crop is the forest
that you did not plant,
that you will not live to harvest
Say that the leaves are harvested
when they have rotted into the mold.
Call that profit. Prophesy such returns.
Put your faith in the two inches of humus

that will build under the trees
every thousand years.
Listen to carrion—put your ear
close, and hear the faint chattering
of the songs that are to come.
Expect the end of the world. Laugh.
Laughter is immeasurable. Be joyful
though you have considered all the facts.
So long as women do not go cheap
for power, please women more than men.
Ask yourself: Will this satisfy
a woman satisfied to bear a child?
Will this disturb the sleep
of a woman near to giving birth?
Go with your love to the fields.
Lie easy in the shade. Rest your head
in her lap. Swear allegiance
to what is nighest your thoughts.
As soon as the generals and the politicos
can predict the motions of your mind,
lose it. Leave it as a sign
to mark a false trail, the way
you didn't go. Be like the fox
who makes more tracks than necessary,
some in the wrong direction.
Practice resurrection.

# THE MAD FARMER MANIFESTO:
# THE FIRST AMENDMENT

*. . . it is not too soon to provide by every*
*possible means that as few as possible shall be*
*without a little portion of land. The small*
*landholders are the most precious part of a state.*

Thomas Jefferson, to Reverend James Madison,
October 28, 1785.

### 1.

That is the glimmering vein
of our sanity, dividing from us
from the start: land under us
to steady us when we stood,
free men in the great communion
of the free. The vision keeps
lighting in my mind, a window
on the horizon in the dark.

### 2.

To be sane in a mad time
is bad for the brain, worse
for the heart. The world
is a holy vision, had we clarity
to see it—a clarity that men
depend on men to make.

### 3.

It is *ignorant* money I declare
myself free from, money fat
and dreaming in its sums, driving
us into the streets of absence,
stranding the pasture trees
in the deserted language of banks.

4.

And I declare myself free
from ignorant love. You easy lovers
and forgivers of mankind, stand back!
I will love you at a distance,
and not because you deserve it.
My love must be discriminate
or fail to bear its weight.


## THE WILD GEESE

Horseback on Sunday morning,
harvest over, we taste persimmon
and wild grape, sharp sweet
of summer's end. In time's maze
over the fall fields, we name names
that went west from here, names
that rest on graves. We open
a persimmon seed to find the tree
that stands in promise,
pale, in the seed's marrow.
Geese appear high over us,
pass, and the sky closes. Abandon,
as in love or sleep, holds
them to their way, clear,
in the ancient faith: what we need
is here. And we pray, not
for new earth or heaven, but to be
quiet in heart, and in eye
clear. What we need is here.

# At a Country Funeral

Now the old ways that have brought us
farther than we remember sink out of sight
as under the treading of many strangers
ignorant of landmarks. Only once in a while
they are cast clear again upon the mind
as at a country funeral where, amid the soft
lights and hothouse flowers, the expensive
solemnity of experts, notes of a polite musician,
persist the usages of old neighborhood.
Friends and kinsmen come and stand and speak,
knowing the extremity they have come to,
one of their own bearing to the earth the last
of his light, his darkness the sun's definitive mark.
They stand and think as they stood and thought
when even the gods were different.
And the organ music, though decorous
as for somebody else's grief, has its source
in the outcry of pain and hope in log churches,
and on naked hillsides by the open grave,
eastward in mountain passes, in tidelands,
and across the sea. How long a time?
Rock of Ages, cleft for me, let me hide my
self in Thee. They came, once in time,
in simple loyalty to their dead, and returned
to the world. The fields and the work
remained to be returned to. Now the entrance
of one of the old ones into the Rock
too often means a lifework perished from the land
without inheritor, and the field goes wild
and the house sits and stares. Or it passes
at cash value into the hands of strangers.
Now the old dead wait in the open coffin
for the blood kin to gather, come home

for one last time, to hear old men
whose tongues bear an essential topography
speak memories doomed to die.
But our memory of ourselves, hard earned,
is one of the land's seeds, as a seed
is the memory of the life of its kind in its place,
to pass on into life the knowledge
of what has died. What we owe the future
is not a new start, for we can only begin
with what has happened. We owe the future
the past, the long knowledge
that is the potency of time to come.
That makes of a man's grave a rich furrow.
The community of knowing in common is the seed
of our life in this place. There is not only
no better possibility, there is no
other, except for chaos and darkness,
the terrible ground of the only possible
new start. And so as the old die and the young
depart, where shall a man go who keeps
the memories of the dead, except home
again, as one would go back after a burial,
faithful to the fields, lest the dead die
a second and more final death.

# TESTAMENT

*And now to the Abyss I pass*
*Of that Unfathomable Grass...*

### 1.

Dear relatives and friends, when my last breath
Grows large and free in air, don't call it death—
A word to enrich the undertaker and inspire
His surly art of imitating life; conspire
Against him. Say that my body cannot now
Be improved upon; it has no fault to show
To the sly cosmetician. Say that my flesh
Has a perfection in compliance with the grass
Truer than any it could have striven for.
You will recognize the earth in me, as before
I wished to know it in myself: my earth
That has been my care and faithful charge from birth,
And toward which all my sorrows were surely bound,
And all my hopes. Say that I have found
A good solution, and am on my way
To the roots. And say I have left my native clay
At last, to be a traveler; that too will be so.
Traveler to where? Say you don't know.

### 2.

But do not let your ignorance
Of my spirit's whereabouts dismay
You, or overwhelm your thoughts.
Be careful not to say

Anything too final. Whatever
Is unsure is possible, and life is bigger

Than flesh. Beyond reach of thought
Let imagination figure

Your hope. That will be generous
To me and to yourselves. Why settle
For some know-it-all's despair
When the dead may dance to the fiddle

Hereafter, for all anybody knows?
And remember that the Heavenly soil
Need not be too rich to please
One who was happy in Port Royal.

I may be already heading back,
A new and better man, toward
That town. The thought's unreasonable,
But so is life, thank the Lord!


3.

So treat me, even dead,
As a man who has a place
To go, and something to do.
Don't muck up my face

With wax and powder and rouge
As one would prettify
An unalterable fact
To give bitterness the lie.

Admit the native earth
My body is and will be,
Admit its freedom and
Its changeability.

Dress me in the clothes
I wore in the day's round.
Lay me in a wooden box.
Put the box in the ground.


4.

Beneath this stone a Berry is planted
In his home land, as he wanted.

He has come to the gathering of his kin,
Among whom some were worthy men,

Farmers mostly, who lived by hand,
But one was a cobbler from Ireland,

Another played the eternal fool
By riding on a circus mule

To be remembered in grateful laughter
Longer than the rest. After

Doing what they had to do
They are at ease here. Let all of you

Who yet for pain find force and voice
Look on their peace, and rejoice.

# The Clear Days
### for Allen Tate

The dogs of indecision
Cross and cross the field of vision.

A cloud, a buzzing fly
Distract the lover's eye.

Until the heart has found
Its native piece of ground.

The day withholds its light,
The eye must stray unlit.

The ground's the body's bride,
Who will not be denied.

Not until all is given
Comes the thought of heaven.

When the mind's an empty room
The clear days come.

*from* Clearing

# History

*For Wallace Stegner*

### 1.

The crops were made, the leaves
were down, three frosts had lain
upon the broad stone
step beneath the door;
as I walked away
the houses were shut, quiet
under their drifting smokes,
the women stooped at the hearths.
Beyond the farthest tracks
of any domestic beast
my way led me, into
a place for which I knew
no names. I went by paths
that bespoke intelligence
and memory I did not know.
Noonday held sounds of moving
water, moving air, enormous
stillness of old trees.
Though I was weary and alone,
song was near me then,
wordless and gay as a deer
lightly stepping. Learning
the landmarks and the ways
of that land, so I might
go back, if I wanted to,
my mind grew new, and lost
the backward way. I stood
at last, long hunter and child,
where this valley opened,
a word I seemed to know

though I had not heard it.
Behind me, along the crooks
and slants of my approach,
a low song sang itself,
as patient as the light.
On the valley floor the woods
grew rich: great poplars,
beeches, sycamores,
walnuts, sweet gums, lindens
oaks. They stood apart
and open, the winter light
at rest among them. Yes,
and as I came down
I heard a little stream
pouring into the river.


    2.

Since then I have arrived here
many times. I have come
on foot, on horseback, by boat,
and by machine—by earth,
water, air, and fire.
I came with axe and rifle.
I came with a sharp eye
and the price of land. I came
in bondage, and I came
in freedom not worth the name.
From the high outlook
of that first day I have come
down two hundred years
across the worked and wasted
slopes, by eroding tracks
of the joyless horsepower of greed.
Through my history's despite

and ruin, I have come
to its remainder, and here
have made the beginning
of a farm intended to become
my art of being here.
By it I would instruct
my wants: they should belong
to one another and to this place.
Until my song comes here
to learn its words, my art
is but the hope of song.


3.

All the lives this place
has had, I have. I eat
my history day by day.
Bird, butterfly, and flower
pass through the seasons of
my flesh. I dine and thrive
on offal and old stone,
and am combined within
the story of the ground.
By this earth's life, I have
its greed and innocence,
its violence, its peace.
Now let me feed my song
upon the life that is here
that is the life that is gone.
This blood has turned to dust
and liquefied again in stem
and vein ten thousand times.
Let what is in the flesh,
O Muse, be brought to mind.

# A Vision

If we will have the wisdom to survive,
to stand like slow-growing trees
on a ruined place, renewing, enriching it,
if we will make our seasons welcome here,
asking not too much of earth or heaven,
then a long time after we are dead
the lives our lives prepare will live
here, their houses strongly placed
upon the valley sides, fields and gardens
rich in the windows. The river will run
clear, as we will never know it,
and over it, birdsong like a canopy.
On the levels of the hills will be
green meadows, stock bells in noon shade.
On the steeps where greed and ignorance cut down
the old forest, an old forest will stand,
its rich leaf-fall drifting on its roots.
The veins of forgotten springs will have opened.
Families will be singing in the fields.
In their voices they will hear a music
risen out of the ground. They will take
nothing from the ground they will not return,
whatever the grief at parting. Memory,
native to this valley, will spread over it
like a grove, and memory will grow
into legend, legend into song, song
into sacrament. The abundance of this place,
the songs of its people and its birds,
will be health and wisdom and indwelling
light. This is no paradisal dream.
Its hardship is its possibility.

*from* A Part

## STAY HOME

I will wait here in the fields
to see how well the rain
brings on the grass.
In the labor of the fields
longer than a man's life
I am at home. Don't come with me.
You stay home too.

I will be standing in the woods
where the old trees
move only with the wind
and then with gravity.
In the stillness of the trees
I am at home. Don't come with me.
You stay home too.

## THE COLD PANE

Between the living world
and the world of death
is a clear, cold pane;
a man who looks too close
must fog it with his breath,
or hold his breath too long.

# For the Hog Killing

Let them stand still for the bullet, and stare the shooter in the
      eye,
let them die while the sound of the shot is in the air, let them die
      as they fall,
let the jugular blood spring hot to the knife, let its freshet be full,
let this day begin again the change of hogs into people, not the
      other way around,
for today we celebrate again our lives' wedding with the world,
for by our hunger, by this provisioning, we renew the bond.

# A Dance

The stepping-stones, once
in a row along the slope,
have drifted out of line,
pushed by frosts and rains.
Walking is no longer thoughtless
over them, but alert as dancing,
as tense and poised, to step
short, and long, and then
longer, right, and then left.
At the winter's end, I dance
the history of its weather.

# The Fear of Love

I come to the fear of love
as I have often come,
to what must be desired
and to what must be done.

Only love can quiet the fear
of love, and only love can save
from diminishment the love
that we must lose to have.

We stand as in an open field,
blossom, leaf, and stem,
rooted and shaken in our day,
heads nodding in the wind.

# To the Holy Spirit

O Thou, far off and here, whole and broken,
Who in necessity and in bounty wait,
Whose truth is light and dark, mute though spoken,
By Thy wide grace show me Thy narrow gate.

## TO WHAT LISTENS

I come to it again
and again, the thought of the wren
opening his song here
to no human ear—
no woman to look up,
no man to turn his head.
The farm will sink then
from all we have done and said.
Beauty will lie, fold
on fold, upon it. Foreseeing
it so, I cannot withhold
love. But from the height
and distance of foresight,
how well I like it
as it is! The river shining,
the bare trees on the bank,
the house set snug
as a stone in the hill's flank,
the pasture behind it green.
Its songs and loves throb
in my head till like the wren
I sing—to what listens—again.

# The Lilies

Hunting them, a man must sweat, bear
the whine of a mosquito in his ear,
grow thirsty, tired, despair perhaps
of ever finding them, walk a long way.
He must give himself over to chance,
for they live beyond prediction.
He must give himself over to patience,
for they live beyond will. He must be led
along the hill as by a prayer.
If he finds them anywhere, he will find
a few, paired on their stalks,
at ease in the air as souls in bliss.
I found them here at first without hunting,
by grace, as all beauties are first found.
I have hunted and not found them here.
Found, unfound, they breathe their light
into the mind, year after year.


# The First

The first man who whistled
thought he had a wren in his mouth.
He went around all day
with his lips puckered,
afraid to swallow.

# BELOW

Above trees and rooftops
is the range of symbols:
banner, cross, and star;
air war, the mode of those
who live by symbols; the pure
abstraction of travel by air.
Here a spire holds up
an angel with trump and wings;
he's in *his* element.
Another lifts a hand
with forefinger pointing up
to admonish that all's not here.
All's not. But I aspire
downward. Flyers embrace
the air, and I'm a man
who needs something to hug.
All my dawns cross the horizon
and rise, from underfoot.
What I stand for
is what I stand on.

# THE HIDDEN SINGER

The gods are less
for their love of praise.
Above and below them all
is a spirit that needs
nothing but its own
wholeness,
its health and ours.
It has made all things
by dividing itself.
It will be whole again.
To its joy we come
together—the seer
and the seen, the eater
and the eaten, the lover
and the loved.
In our joining it knows
itself. It is with us then,
not as the gods
whose names crest
in unearthly fire,
but as a little bird
hidden in the leaves
who sings quietly
and waits
and sings.

# Ripening

The longer we are together
the larger death grows around us.
How many we know by now
who are dead! We, who were young,
now count the cost of having been.
And yet as we know the dead
we grow familiar with the world.
We, who were young and loved each other
ignorantly, now come to know
each other in love, married
by what we have done, as much
as by what we intend. Our hair
turns white with our ripening
as though to fly away in some
coming wind, bearing the seed
of what we know. It was bitter to learn
that we come to death as we come
to love, bitter to face
the just and solving welcome
that death prepares. But that is bitter
only to the ignorant, who pray
it will not happen. Having come
the bitter way to better prayer, we have
the sweetness of ripening. How sweet
to know you by the signs of this world!

# The Way of Pain

### 1.

For parents, the only way
is hard. We who give life
give pain. There is no help.
Yet we who give pain
give love; by pain we learn
the extremity of love.

### 2.

I read of Abraham's sacrifice
the Voice required of him,
so that he led to the altar
and the knife his only son.
The beloved life was spared
that time, but not the pain.
It was the pain that was required.

### 3.

I read of Christ crucified,
the only begotten Son
sacrificed to flesh and time
and all our woe. He died
and rose, but who does not tremble
for his pain, his loneliness,
and the darkness of the sixth hour?
Unless we grieve like Mary
at His grave, giving Him up
as lost, no Easter morning comes.

### 4.

And then I slept, and dreamed
the life of my only son
was required of me, and I

must bring him to the edge
of pain, not knowing why.
I woke, and yet that pain
was true. It brought his life
to the full in me. I bore him
suffering, with love like the sun,
too bright, unsparing, whole.


## A Meeting

In a dream I meet
my dead friend. He has,
I know, gone long and far,
and yet he is the same
for the dead are changeless.
They grow no older.
It is I who have changed,
grown strange to what I was.
Yet I, the changed one,
ask: "How you been?"
He grins and looks at me.
"I been eating peaches
off some mighty fine trees."

## We Who Prayed and Wept

We who prayed and wept
for liberty from kings
and the yoke of liberty
accept the tyranny of things
we do not need.
In plenitude too free,
we have become adept
beneath the yoke of greed.

Those who will not learn
in plenty to keep their place
must learn it by their need
when they have had their way
and the fields spurn their seed.
We have failed Thy grace.
Lord, I flinch and pray,
send Thy necessity.

## Traveling at Home

Even in a country you know by heart
it's hard to go the same way twice.
The life of the going changes.
The chances change and make a new way.
Any tree or stone or bird
can be the bud of a new direction. The
natural correction is to make intent
of accident. To get back before dark
is the art of going.

# GRIEF

The morning comes. The old woman, a spot
of soot where she has touched her cheek, tears
on her face, builds a fire, sets water to boil,
puts the skillet on. The man in his middle years,
bent by the work he has done toward the work
he will do, weeps as he eats, bread in his mouth,
tears on his face. They shape the day for its passing
as if absent from it—for what needs care, caring,
feeding what must be fed. To keep them, there are only
the household's remembered ways, etched thin
and brittle by their tears. It is a sharp light
that lights the day now. It seems to shine,
beyond eyesight, also in another day
where the dead have risen and are walking
away, their backs forever turned. What
look is in their eyes? What do they say
as they walk into the fall and flow of light?
It seems that they must know where they are going.
And the living must go with them, not knowing,
a little way. And the dead go on, not turning,
knowing, but not saying. And the living
turn back to their day, their grieving and staying.

# A Warning to My Readers

Do not think me gentle
because I speak in praise
of gentleness, or elegant
because I honor the grace
that keeps this world. I am
a man crude as any,
gross of speech, intolerant,
stubborn, angry, full
of fits and furies. That I
may have spoken well
at times is not natural.
A wonder is what it is.

# Throwing Away the Mail

Nothing is simple,
not even simplification.

Thus, throwing away
the mail, I exchange
the complexity of duty
for the simplicity of guilt.

# CREATION MYTH

This is a story handed down.
It is about the old days when Bill
and Florence and a lot of their kin
lived in the little tin-roofed house
beside the woods, below the hill.
Mornings, they went up the hill
to work, Florence to the house,
the men and boys to the field.
Evenings, they all came home again.
There would be talk then and laughter
and taking of ease around the porch
while the summer night closed.
But one night, McKinley, Bill's young brother,
stayed away late, and it was dark
when he started down the hill.
Not a star shone, not a window.
What he was going down into was
the dark, only his footsteps sounding
to prove he trod the ground. And Bill
who had got up to cool himself,
thinking and smoking, leaning on
the jamb of the open front door,
heard McKinley coming down,
and heard his steps beat faster
as he came, for McKinley felt the pasture's
darkness joined to all the rest
of darkness everywhere. It touched
the depths of woods and sky and grave.
In that huge dark, things that usually
stayed put might get around, as fish
in pond or slue get loose in flood.
Oh, things could be coming close

that never had come close before.
He missed the house and went on down
and crossed the draw and pounded on
where the pasture widened on the other side,
lost then for sure. Propped in the door,
Bill heard him circling, a dark star
in the dark, breathing hard, his feet
blind on the little reality
that was left. Amused, Bill smoked
his smoke, and listened. He knew where
McKinley was, though McKinley didn't.
Bill smiled in the darkness to himself,
and let McKinley run until his steps
approached something really to fear:
the quarry pool. Bill quit his pipe
then, opened the screen, and stepped out,
barefoot, on the warm boards. "McKinley!"
he said, and laid the field out clear
under McKinley's feet, and placed
the map of it in his head.

## Except

Now that you have gone
and I am alone and quiet,
my contentment would be
complete, if I did not wish
you were here so I could say,
"How good it is, Tanya,
to be alone and quiet."

# THE SLIP
### for Donald Davie

The river takes the land, and leaves nothing.
Where the great slip gave way in the bank
and an acre disappeared, all human plans
dissolve. An awful clarification occurs
where a place was. Its memory breaks
from what is known now, begins to drift.
Where cattle grazed and trees stood, emptiness
widens the air for birdflight, wind, and rain.
As before the beginning, nothing is there.
Human wrong is in the cause, human
ruin in the effect—but no matter;
all will be lost, no matter the reason.
Nothing, having arrived, will stay.
The earth, even, is like a flower, so soon
passeth it away. And yet this nothing
is the seed of all—the clear eye
of Heaven, where all the worlds appear.
Where the imperfect has departed, the perfect
begins its struggle to return. The good gift
begins again its descent. The maker moves
in the unmade, stirring the water until
it clouds, dark beneath the surface,
stirring and darkening the soul until pain
perceives new possibility. There is nothing
to do but learn and wait, return to work
on what remains. Seed will sprout in the scar.
Though death is in the healing, it will heal.

# Horses

When I was a boy here,
traveling the fields for pleasure,
the farms were worked with teams.
As late as then a teamster
was thought an accomplished man,
his art an essential discipline.
A boy learned it by delight
as he learned to use
his body, following the example
of men. The reins of a team
were put into my hands
when I thought the work was play.
And in the corrective gaze
of men now dead I learned
to flesh my will in power
great enough to kill me
should I let it turn.
I learned the other tongue
by which men spoke to beasts
—all its terms and tones.
And by the time I learned,
new ways had changed the time.
The tractors came. The horses
stood in the fields, keepsakes,
grew old, and died. Or were sold
as dogmeat. Our minds received
the revolution of engines, our will
stretched toward the numb endurance
of metal. And that old speech
by which we magnified
our flesh in other flesh
fell dead in our mouths.

The songs of the world died
in our ears as we went within
the uproar of the long syllable
of the motors. Our intent entered
the world as combustion.
Like our travels, our workdays
burned upon the world,
lifting its inwards up
in fire. Veiled in that power
our minds gave up the endless
cycle of growth and decay
and took the unreturning way,
the breathless distance of iron.

But that work, empowered by burning
the world's body, showed us
finally the world's limits
and our own. We had then
the life of a candle, no longer
the ever-returning song
among the grassblades and the leaves.

Did I never forget?
Or did I, after years,
remember? To hear that song
again, though brokenly
in the distances of memory,
is coming home. I came to
a farm, some of it unreachable
by machines, as some of the world
will always be. And so
I came to a team, a pair
of mares—sorrels, with white
tails and manes, beautiful!—

to keep my sloping fields.
Going behind them, the reins
tight over their backs as they stepped
their long strides, revived
again on my tongue the cries
of dead men in the living
fields. Now every move
answers what is still.
This work of love rhymes
living and dead. A dance
is what this plodding is.
A song, whatever is said.

*from* The Wheel

# Requiem

*Owen Flood / January 13, 1920–March 27, 1974*

### 1.

We will see no more
the mown grass fallen behind him
on the still ridges before night,
or hear him laughing in the crop rows,
or know the order of his delight.

Though the green fields are my delight,
elegy is my fate. I have come to be
survivor of many and of much
that I love, that I won't live to see
come again into this world.

Things that mattered to me once
won't matter any more,
for I have left the safe shore
where magnificence of art
could suffice my heart.

### 2.

In the day of his work
when the grace of the world
was upon him, he made his way,
not turning back or looking aside,
light in his stride.

Now may the grace of death
be upon him, his spirit blessed
in deep song of the world
and the stars turning, the seasons
returning, and long rest.

# ELEGY

To be at home on its native ground
the mind must go down below its horizon,
descend below the lightfall
on ridge and steep and valley floor
to receive the lives of the dead. It must wake
in their sleep, who wake in its dreams.

"Who is here?" On the rock road between
creek and woods in the fall of the year,
I stood and listened. I heard the cries
of little birds high in the wind.
And then the beat of old footsteps
came around me, and my sight was changed.

I passed through the lens of darkness
as through a furrow, and the dead
gathered to meet me. They knew me,
but looked in wonder at the lines in my face,
the white hairs sprinkled on my head.

I saw a tall old man leaning
upon a cane, his open hand
raised in some fierce commendation,
knowledge of long labor in his eyes;
another, a gentler countenance,
smiling beneath a brim of sweaty felt
in welcome to me as before.

I saw an old woman, a saver
of little things, whose lonely grief
was the first I knew; and one bent

with age and pain, whose busy hands
worked out a selflessness of love.

Those were my teachers. And there were more,
beloved of face and name, who once bore
the substance of our common ground.
Their eyes, having grieved all grief, were clear.

2.
I saw one standing aside, alone,
weariness in his shoulders, his eyes
bewildered yet with the newness
of his death. In my sorrow I felt,
as many times before, gladness
at the sight of him. "Owen," I said.

He turned—lifted, tilted his hand.
I handed him a clod of earth
picked up in a certain well-known field.
He kneaded it in his palm and spoke:
"Wendell, this is not a place
for you and me." And then he grinned;
we recognized his stubbornness—
it was his principle to doubt
all ease of satisfaction.

"The crops are in the barn," I said,
"the morning frost has come to the fields,
and I have turned back to accept,
if I can, what none of us could prevent."

He stood, remembering, weighing the cost
of the division we had come to,
his fingers resting on the earth

he held cupped lightly in his palm.
It seemed to me then that he cast off
his own confusion, and assumed
for one last time, in one last kindness,
the duty of the older man.

He nodded his head. "The desire I had
in early morning and in spring,
I never wore it out. I had
the desire, if I had had the strength.
But listen—what we prepared
to have, we have."

                    He raised his eyes.
"Look," he said.


        3.
                    We stood on a height,
woods above us, and below
on the half-mowed slope we saw ourselves
as we once were: a young man mowing,
a boy grubbing with an axe.

It was an old abandoned field,
long overgrown with thorns and briars.
We made it new in the heat haze
of that midsummer: he, proud
of the ground intelligence clarified,
and I, proud in his praise.

"I wish," I said, "that we could be
back in that good time again."

"We are back there again, today
and always. Where else would we be?"
He smiled, looked at me, and I knew
it was my mind he led me through.
He spoke of some infinitude
of thought.

He led me to another
slope beside another woods,
this lighted only by stars. Older
now, the man and the boy lay
on their backs in deep grass, quietly
talking. In the distance moved
the outcry of one deep-voiced hound.

Other voices joined that voice:
another place, a later time,
a hunter's fire among the trees,
faces turned to the blaze, laughter
and then silence, while in the dark
around us lay long breaths of sleep.

4.
And then, one by one, he moved me
through all the fields of our lives,
preparations, plantings, harvests,
crews joking at the row ends,
the water jug passing like a kiss.

He spoke of our history passing through us,
the way our families' generations
overlap, the great teaching
coming down by deed of companionship:

characters of fields and times and men,
qualities of devotion and of work—
endless fascinations, passions
old as mind, new as light.

All our years around us, near us,
I saw him furious and narrow,
like most men, and saw the virtue
that made him unlike most.
It was his passion to be true
to the condition of the Fall—
to live by the sweat of his face, to eat
his bread, assured that cost was paid.

5.

We came then to his time of pain,
when the early morning light showed,
as always, the sweet world, and all
an able, well-intentioned man
might do by dark, and his strength failed
before the light. His body had begun
too soon its earthward journey,
filling with gravity, and yet his mind
kept its old way.

                    Again, in the sun
of his last harvest, I heard him say:
"Do you want to take this row,
and let me get out of your way?"
I saw the world ahead of him then
for the first time, and I saw it
as he already had seen it,
himself gone from it. It was a sight
I could not see and not weep.

He reached and would have touched me
with his hand, though he could not.


6.
Finally, he brought me to a hill
overlooking the fields that once
belonged to him, that he once
belonged to. "Look," he said again.
I knew he wanted me to see
the years of care that place wore,
for his story lay upon it, a bloom,
a blessing.

          The time and place so near,
we almost were the men we watched.
Summer's end sang in the light.
We spoke of death and obligation,
the brevity of things and men.
Words never moved so heavily
between us, or cost us more. We hushed.
And then that man who bore his death
in him, and knew it, quietly said:
"Well. It's a fascinating world,
after all."

          His life so powerfully
stood there in presence of his place
and work and time, I could not
realize except with grief
that only his spirit now was with me.


In the very hour he died, I told him,
before I knew his death, the thought
of years to come had moved me

like a call. I thought of healing,
health, friendship going on,
the generations gathering, our good times
reaching one best time of all.


    7.
My mind was overborne with questions
I could not speak. It seemed to me
we had returned now to the dark
valley where our journey began.
But a brightening intelligence
was on his face. Insight moved him
as he once was moved by daylight.


The best teachers teach more
than they know. By their deaths
they teach most. They lead us beyond
what we know, and what they knew.
Thus my teacher, my old friend,
stood smiling now before me, wholly
moved by what had moved him partly
in the world.

                      Again the host of the dead
encircled us, as in a dance.
And I was aware now of the unborn
moving among them. As they turned
I could see their bodies come to light
and fade again in the dark throng.
They moved as to a distant or a hovering
song I strained for, but could not hear.


"Our way is endless," my teacher said.
"The Creator is divided in Creation

for the joys of recognition. We knew
that Spirit in each other once;
it brings us here. By its divisions
and returns, the world lives.
Both mind and earth are made
of what its light gives and uses up.
So joy contains, survives its cost.
The dead abide, as grief knows.
We are what we have lost."

There is a song in the Creation;
it has always been the gift
of every gifted voice, though none
ever sang it. As he spoke
I heard that song. In its changes and returns
his life was passing into life.
That moment, earth and song and mind,
the living and the dead, were one.

        8.
At last, completed in his rest,
as one who has worked and bathed, fed
and loved and slept, he let fall
the beloved earth that I had brought him.
He raised his hand, turned me to my way.
And I, inheritor of what I mourned,
went back toward the light of day.

# The Law That Marries All Things

### 1.

The cloud is free only
to go with the wind.

The rain is free
only in falling.

The water is free only
in its gathering together,

in its downward courses,
in its rising into air.

### 2.

In law is rest
if you love the law,
if you enter, singing, into it
as water in its descent.

### 3.

Or song is truest law,
and you must enter singing;
it has no other entrance.

It is the great chorus
of parts. The only outlawry
is in division.

### 4.

Whatever is singing
is found, awaiting the return
of whatever is lost.

5.

Meet us in the air
over the water,
sing the swallows.

Meet me, meet me,
the redbird sings,
here here here here.



## Song

I stood and heard the steps of the city
and dreamed a lighter stepping than I heard,
the tread of my people dancing in a ring.
I knew that circle broken, the steps awry,
stone and iron humming in the air.

But I thought even there, among the straying
steps, of the dance that circles life around,
its shadows moving on the ground, in rhyme
of flesh with flesh, time with time, our bliss,
the earthly song that heavenly is.

# From the Distance

### 1.

We are others and the earth,
the living of the dead.
Remembering who we are,
we live in eternity;
any solitary act
is work of community.

### 2.

All times are one
if hearts delight
in work, if hands
join the world right.

### 3.

The wheel of eternity is turning
in time, its rhymes, austere,
at long intervals returning,
sing in the mind, not in the ear.

### 4.

A man of faithful thought may feel
in light, among the beasts and fields,
the turning of the wheel.

### 5.

Fall of the year:
at evening a frail mist
rose, glowing in the rain.
The dead and unborn drew near
the fire. A song, not mine,
stuttered in the flame.

# THE GIFT OF GRAVITY

All that passes descends,
and ascends again unseen
into the light: the river
coming down from sky
to hills, from hills to sea,
and carving as it moves,
to rise invisible,
gathered to light, to return
again. "The river's injury
is its shape." I've learned no more.
We are what we are given
and what is taken away;
blessed be the name
of the giver and taker.
For everything that comes
is a gift, the meaning always
carried out of sight
to renew our whereabouts,
always a starting place.
And every gift is perfect
in its beginning, for it
is "from above, and cometh down
from the Father of lights."
Gravity is grace.
All that has come to us
has come as the river comes,
given in passing away.
And if our wickedness
destroys the watershed,
dissolves the beautiful field,
then I must grieve and learn
that I possess by loss

the earth I live upon
and stand in and am. The dark
and then the light will have it.
I am newborn of pain
to love the new-shaped shore
where young cottonwoods
take hold and thrive in the wound,
kingfishers already nesting
in a hole in the sheared bank.
"What is left is what is"—
have learned no more. The shore
turns green under the songs
of the fires of the world's end,
and what is there to do?
Imagine what exists
so that it may shine
in thought light and day light,
lifted up in the mind.
The dark returns to light
in the kingfisher's blue and white
richly laid together.
He falls into flight
from the broken ground,
with strident outcry gathers
air under his wings.
In work of love, the body
forgets its weight. And once
again with love and singing
in mind, I come to what
must come to me, carried
as a dancer by a song.
This grace is gravity.

# THE WHEEL
### for Robert Penn Warren

At the first strokes of the fiddle bow
the dancers rise from their seats.
The dance begins to shape itself
in the crowd, as couples join,
and couples join couples, their movement
together lightening their feet.
They move in the ancient circle
of the dance. The dance and the song
call each other into being. Soon
they are one—rapt in a single
rapture, so that even the night
has its clarity, and time
is the wheel that brings it round.
In this rapture the dead return.
Sorrow is gone from them.
They are light. They step
into the steps of the living
and turn with them in the dance
in the sweet enclosure
of the song, and timeless
is the wheel that brings it round.

# Our Children, Coming of Age

In the great circle, dancing in
and out of time, you move now
toward your partners, answering
the music suddenly audible to you
that only carried you before
and will carry you again.
When you meet the destined ones
now dancing toward you,
we will be in line behind you,
out of your awareness for the time,
we whom you know, others we remember
whom you do not remember, others
forgotten by us all.
When you meet, and hold love
in your arms, regardless of all,
the unknown will dance away from you
toward the horizon of light.
Our names will flutter
on these hills like little fires.

# Song

*for Guy Davenport*

Within the circles of our lives
we dance the circles of the years,
the circles of the seasons
within the circles of the years,
the cycles of the moon
within the circles of the seasons,
the circles of our reasons
within the cycles of the moon.

Again, again we come and go,
changed, changing. Hands
join, unjoin in love and fear,
grief and joy. The circles turn,
each giving into each, into all.
Only music keeps us here,

each by all the others held.
In the hold of hands and eyes
we turn in pairs, that joining
joining each to all again.

And then we turn aside, alone,
out of the sunlight gone

into the darker circles of return.

# In Rain

### 1.

I go in under foliage
light with rain-light
in the hill's cleft,
and climb, my steps
silent as flight
on the wet leaves.
Where I go, stones
are wearing away
under the sky's flow.

### 2.

The path I follow
I can hardly see
it is so faintly trod
and overgrown.
At times, looking,
I fail to find it
among dark trunks, leaves
living and dead. And then
I am alone, the woods
shapeless around me.
I look away, my gaze
at rest among leaves,
and then I see the path
again, a dark way going
on through the light.

### 3.

In a mist of light
falling with the rain
I walk this ground

of which dead men
and women I have loved
are part, as they
are part of me. In earth,
in blood, in mind,
the dead and living
into each other pass,
as the living pass
in and out of loves
as stepping to a song.
The way I go is
marriage to this place,
grace beyond chance,
love's braided dance
covering the world.

4.

Marriages to marriages
are joined, husband and wife
are plighted to all
husbands and wives,
any life has all lives
for its delight.
Let the rain come,
the sun, and then the dark,
for I will rest
in an easy bed tonight.

*from* Entries

## For the Explainers

Spell the spiel of cause and effect,
Ride the long rail of fact after fact;
What curled the plume in the drake's tail
And put the white ring round his neck?


## Epitaph

Having lived long in time,
he lives now in timelessness
without sorrow, made perfect
by our never finished love,
by our compassion and forgiveness,
and by his happiness in receiving
these gifts we give. Here in time
we are added to one another forever.

# A Marriage Song

In January cold, the year's short light,
We make new marriage here;
The day is clear, the ground is bridal white,
Songless the brittled air
As we come through the snow to praise
Our Mary in her day of days.

In time's short light, and less than light, we pray
That odds be thus made evens,
And earthly love in its uncertain way
Be reconciled with Heaven's.
Before the early dark, we praise
Our Mary in her day of days.

Now let her honest, honored bridegroom come,
All other choice foregone,
To make his vows and claim and take her home,
Their two lives made in one.
He comes now through the snow to praise
Our Mary in her day of days.

All preparation past, and rightly glad,
She makes her pledge for good
Against all possibility of bad,
Begins her womanhood,
And as she walks the snow, we praise
Our Mary in her day of days.

Now, as her parents, we must stand aside,
For what we owed we've paid her
In far from perfect truth and love—this bride
Is more than we have made her,
And so we come in snow to praise
Our Mary in her day of days.

*January 10, 1981*

## THIRTY MORE YEARS

When I was a young man,
grown up at last, how large
I seemed to myself! I was a tree,
tall already, and what I had not
yet reached, I would yet grow
to reach. Now, thirty more years
added on, I have reached much
I did not expect, in a direction
unexpected. I am growing downward,
smaller, one among the grasses.

# THE RECORD

My old friend tells us how the country changed:
where the grist mill was on Cane Run,
now gone; where the peach orchard was,
gone too; where the Springport Road was, gone
beneath returning trees; how the creek ran three weeks
after a good rain, long ago, no more;
how when these hillsides first were plowed, the soil
was black and deep, no stones, and that was long ago;
where the wild turkeys roosted in the old days.
"You'd have to know this country mighty well
before I could tell you where."

And my young friend says: "Have him speak this
into a recorder. It is precious. It should be saved."
I know the panic of that wish to save
the vital knowledge of the old times, handed down,
for it is rising off the earth, fraying away
in the wind and the coming day.
As the machines come and the people go
the old names rise, chattering, and depart.

But knowledge of my own going into old time
tells me no. Because it must be saved,
do not tell it to a machine to save it.
That old man speaking you have heard
since your boyhood, since his prime, his voice
speaking out of lives long dead, their minds
speaking in his own, by winter fires, in fields and woods,
in barns while rain beat on the roofs
and wind shook the girders. Stay and listen
until he dies or you die, for death
is in this, and grief is in it. Live here

as one who knows these things. Stay, if you live;
listen and answer. Listen to the next one
like him, if there is to be one. Be
the next one like him, if you must.
Stay and wait. Tell your children. Tell them
to tell their children. As you depart
toward the coming light, turn back
and speak, as the creek steps downward
over the rocks, saying the same changing thing
in the same place as it goes.

When the record is made, the unchanging
word carried to a safe place
in a time not here, the assemblage
of minds dead and living, the loved lineage
dispersed, silent, turned away, the dead
dead at last, it will be too late.

## THE WILD ROSE

Sometimes hidden from me
in daily custom and in trust,
so that I live by you unaware
as by the beating of my heart,

suddenly you flare in my sight,
a wild rose blooming at the edge
of thicket, grace and light
where yesterday was only a shade,

and once more I am blessed, choosing
again what I chose before.

# THE BLUE ROBE

How joyful to be together, alone
as when we first were joined
in our little house by the river
long ago, except that now we know

each other, as we did not then;
and now instead of two stories fumbling
to meet, we belong to one story
that the two, joining, made. And now

we touch each other with the tenderness
of mortals, who know themselves:
how joyful to feel the heart quake

at the sight of a grandmother,
old friend in the morning light,
beautiful in her blue robe!

# IN A MOTEL PARKING LOT,
## THINKING OF DR. WILLIAMS

### I.

The poem is important, but
not more than the people
whose survival it serves,

one of the necessities, so they may
speak what is true, and have
the patience for beauty: the weighted

grainfield, the shady street,
the well-laid stone and the changing tree
whose branches spread above.

For want of songs and stories
they have dug away the soil,
paved over what is left,

set up their perfunctory walls
in tribute to no god,
for the love of no man or woman,

so that the good that was here
cannot be called back
except by long waiting, by great

sorrows remembered and to come,
by invoking the understones
of the world, and the vivid air.

II.

The poem is important,
as the want of it
proves. It is the stewardship

of its own possibility,
the past remembering itself
in the presence of

the present, the power learned
and handed down to see
what is present

and what is not: the pavement
laid down and walked over
regardlessly—by exiles, here

only because they are passing.
Oh, remember the oaks that were
here, the leaves, purple and brown,

falling, the nuthatches walking
headfirst down the trunks,
crying *"onc! onc!"* in the brightness

as they are doing now
in the cemetery across the street
where the past and the dead

keep each other. To remember,
to hear and remember, is to stop
and walk on again

to a livelier, surer measure.
It is dangerous
to remember the past only

for its own sake, dangerous
to deliver a message
you did not get.

## THE VACATION

Once there was a man who filmed his vacation.
He went flying down the river in his boat
with his video camera to his eye, making
a moving picture of the moving river
upon which his sleek boat moved swiftly
toward the end of his vacation. He showed
his vacation to his camera, which pictured it,
preserving it forever: the river, the trees,
the sky, the light, the bow of his rushing boat
behind which he stood with his camera
preserving his vacation even as he was having it
so that after he had had it he would still
have it. It would be there. With a flick
of a switch, there it would be. But he
would not be in it. He would never be in it.

## ANGLO-SAXON PROTESTANT HETEROSEXUAL MEN

Come, dear brothers,
let us cheerfully acknowledge
that we are the last hope of the world,
for we have no excuses,
nobody to blame but ourselves.
Who is going to sit at our feet
and listen while we bewail
our historical sufferings? Who
will ever believe that we also
have wept in the night
with repressed longing to become
our real selves? Who will
stand forth and proclaim
that we have virtues and talents
peculiar to our category? Nobody,
and that is good. For here we are
at last with our real selves
in the real world. Therefore,
let us quiet our hearts, my brothers,
and settle down for a change
to picking up after ourselves
and a few centuries of honest work.

# AIR

This man, proud and young,
turns homeward in the dark
heaven, free of his burden
of death by fire, of life in fear
of death by fire, in the city
now burning far below.

This is a young man, proud;
he sways upon the tall stalk
of pride, alone, in control of the
explosion by which he lives, one
of the children we have taught
to be amused by horror.

This is a proud man, young
in the work of death. Ahead of him
wait those made rich by fire.
Behind him, another child
is burning; a divine man
is hanging from a tree.

# ENEMIES

If you are not to become a monster,
you must care what they think.
If you care what they think,

how will you not hate them,
and so become a monster
of the opposite kind? From where then

is love to come—love for your enemy
that is the way of liberty?
From forgiveness. Forgiven, they go

free of you, and you of them;
they are to you as sunlight
on a green branch. You must not

think of them again, except
as monsters like yourself,
pitiable because unforgiving.

## To My Mother

I was your rebellious son,
do you remember? Sometimes
I wonder if you do remember,
so complete has your forgiveness been.

So complete has your forgiveness been
I wonder sometimes if it did not
precede my wrong, and I erred,
safe found, within your love,

prepared ahead of me, the way home,
or my bed at night, so that almost
I should forgive you, who perhaps
foresaw the worst that I might do,

and forgave before I could act,
causing me to smile now, looking back,
to see how paltry was my worst,
compared to your forgiveness of it

already given. And this, then,
is the vision of that Heaven of which
we have heard, where those who love
each other have forgiven each other,

where, for that, the leaves are green,
the light a music in the air,
and all is unentangled,
and all is undismayed.

## The Mad Farmer, Flying the Flag of Rough Branch, Secedes from the Union

From the union of power and money,
from the union of power and secrecy,
from the union of government and science,
from the union of government and art,
from the union of science and money,
from the union of ambition and ignorance,
from the union of genius and war,
from the union of outer space and inner vacuity,
the Mad Farmer walks quietly away.

There is only one of him, but he goes.
He returns to the small country he calls home,
his own nation small enough to walk across.
He goes shadowy into the local woods,
and brightly into the local meadows and croplands.
He goes to the care of neighbors,
he goes into the care of neighbors.
He goes to the potluck supper, a dish
from each house for the hunger of every house.
He goes into the quiet of early mornings
of days when he is not going anywhere.

Calling his neighbors together into the sanctity
of their lives separate and together
in the one life of their commonwealth and home,
in their own nation small enough for a story
or song to travel across in an hour, he cries:

Come all ye conservatives and liberals
who want to conserve the good things and be free,
come away from the merchants of big answers,

whose hands are metalled with power;
from the union of anywhere and everywhere
by the purchase of everything from everybody at the lowest price
and the sale of anything to anybody at the highest price;
from the union of work and debt, work and despair;
from the wage-slavery of the helplessly well-employed.

From the union of self-gratification and self-annihilation,
secede into care for one another
and for the good gifts of Heaven and Earth.

Come into the life of the body, the one body
granted to you in all the history of time.
Come into the body's economy, its daily work,
and its replenishment at mealtimes and at night.
Come into the body's thanksgiving, when it knows
and acknowledges itself a living soul.
Come into the dance of the community, joined
in a circle, hand in hand, the dance of the eternal
love of women and men for one another
and of neighbors and friends for one another.

Always disappearing, always returning,
calling his neighbors to return, to think again
of the care of flocks and herds, of gardens
and fields, of woodlots and forests and the uncut groves,
calling them separately and together, calling and calling,
he goes forever toward the long restful evening
and the croak of the night heron over the river at dark.

# DUALITY

*So God created man in his*
*own image, in the image of God*
*created he him; male and female*
*created he them.*

### I

To love is to suffer—did I
know this when first
I asked you for your love?
I did not. And yet until
I knew, I could not know what
I asked, or gave. I gave
a suffering that I took: yours
and mine, mine when yours;
and yours I have feared most.

### II

What can bring us past
this knowledge, so that you
will never wish our life
undone? For if ever you
wish it so, then I must wish
so too, and lovers yet unborn,
whom we are reaching toward
with love, will turn to this
page, and find it blank.

### III

I have feared to be unknown
and to offend—I must speak,
then, against the dread

of speech. What if, hearing,
you have no reply, and mind's
despair annul the body's hope?
Life in time may justify
any conclusion, whenever
our will is to conclude.


IV

Look at me now. Now,
after all the years, look at me
who have no beauty apart
from what we two have been
and made. Look at me
with the look that anger
and pain have taught you,
the gaze in which nothing
is guarded, nothing withheld.


V

You look at me, you give
a light, which I bear and return,
and we are held, and all
our time is held, in this
touching look—this touch
that, pressed against the touch
returning in the dark,
is almost sight. We burn
and see by our own light.


VI

Eyes looking into eyes looking
into eyes, touches that see
in the dark, remember Paradise,

our true home. God's image
recalls us to Itself. We move
with motion not our own,
light upon light, day and
night, sway as two trees
in the same wind sway.

VII

Let us come to no conclusion,
but let our bodies burn
in time's timelessness. Heaven
and earth give us to this night
in which we tell each other of
a Kingdom yet to come, saying
its secret, its silent names.
We become fleshed words, one
another's uttered joy.

VIII

Joined in our mortal motion,
we come to the resurrection
of words; they rise up
in our mouths, set free
of taints, errors, and bad luck.
In their new clarities
the leaf brightens, the air
clears, the syllables of water are
clear in the dark air as stars.

IX

We come, unsighted, in the dark,
to the great feast of lovers
where nothing is withheld.

That we are there we know
by touch, by inner sight.
They all are here, who by
their giving take, by taking
give, who by their living
love, and by loving live.


## For an Absence

When I cannot be with you
I will send my love (so much
is allowed to human lovers)
to watch over you in the dark—
a winged small presence
who never sleeps, however long
the night. Perhaps it cannot
protect or help, I do not know,
but it watches always, and so
you will sleep within my love
within the room within the dark.
And when, restless, you wake
and see the room palely lit
by that watching, you will think,
"It is only dawn," and go
quiet to sleep again.

# The Storm

We lay in our bed as in a tomb
awakened by thunder to the dark
in which our house was one with night,
and then light came as if the black
roof of the world had cracked open,
as if the night of all time had broken,
and out our window we glimpsed the world
birthwet and shining, as even
the sun at noon had never made it shine.

# REMEMBERING MY FATHER

What did I learn from him?
He taught the difference
Between good work and sham,
Between nonsense and sense.

He taught me sentences,
Outspoken fact for fact,
In swift coherences
Discriminate and exact.

He served with mind and hand
What we were hoping for:
The small house on the land,
The shade tree by the door,

Garden, smokehouse, and cellar,
Granary, crib, and loft
Abounding, and no year
Lived at the next year's cost.

He kept in mind, alive,
The idea of the dead:
"A steer should graze and thrive
Wherever he lowers his head."

He said his father's saying.
We were standing on the hill
To watch the cattle grazing
As the gray evening fell.

"Look. See that this is good,
And then you won't forget."
I saw it as he said,
And I have not forgot.


## COME FORTH

I dreamed of my father when he was old.
We went to see some horses in a field;
they were sorrels, as red almost as blood,
the light gold on their shoulders and haunches.
Though they came to us, all a-tremble
with curiosity and snorty with caution,
they had never known bridle or harness.
My father walked among them, admiring,
for he was a knower of horses, and these were fine.

He leaned on a cane and dragged his feet
along the ground in hurried little steps
so that I called to him to take care, take care,
as the horses stamped and frolicked around him.
But while I warned, he seized the mane
of the nearest one. "It'll be all right,"
he said, and then from his broken stance
he leapt astride, and sat lithe and straight
and strong in the sun's unshadowed excellence.

# Title Index

# Index of First Lines